THE BRIBE

(Photo by Bernie Fedderson)

THE BRIBE

Philip Ross

HARPER & ROW, PUBLISHERS

New York, Hagerstown, San Francisco, London

B

Ross

FIRST EDITION

Designed by C. Linda Dingler

Library of Congress Cataloging in Publication Data

Ross, Philip, 1939–
    The bribe.
    1. Ross, Burt. 2. Corruption (in politics)—
Fort Lee, N. J. 3. Fort Lee, N. J.—Politics and
government. I. Title.
JS883.F7R67   320.9′749′21   [B]   75-25063
ISBN 0-06-013658-8

76 77 78 79 10 9 8 7 6 5 4 3 2 1

For Joana and Dahlia

To Susan and Mark Haven, Ellen Levine, Rose and David Ross, Laurie Miller and Tana Ross, for what they said.

To Jonathan Goldstein, Bruce Goldstein, Richard Shapiro and the entire U.S. Attorney's office in Newark; to Arthur Dalton and the Fort Lee Police Department; to Bernard Pirog and the scores of FBI agents who worked the case; to Carl Hirschman and the U.S. Marshal's office in Newark; and to L.F. Rothschild & Co., for what they did.

And to Burt Ross, for everything.

THE BRIBE

1

It is a cold and windy Saturday night in March when my father and I arrive for dinner. The evening is meant to be an informal celebration. The trial is still in progress but my brother Burt, a week away from his thirty-second birthday, has just finished on the witness stand. A verdict may be a month off, but there is reason enough to celebrate now. He was terrific.

"Ross: Unflustered and Forthright," the morning paper had headlined.

"All our witnesses should only be like him," the U.S. Attorney prosecuting the case had whispered during a recess.

Yet this dinner tonight is not so much to pay tribute to a great performance as it is to take quiet pleasure in the fact that the curtain itself has finally fallen. For Burt, at least, it's over now. Ten months of FBI and staked-out restaurants, hidden mikes and recording equipment, U.S. marshals and Tommy guns, threats on his life and country hideouts. It's all over. And we have come to drink to that. To survival as much as to success.

The front door of Bill and Joanne Miller's Long Island house is partly open and we walk in without knocking. Joanne Miller, Burt's mother-in-law, is sitting on a couch next to an elaborately set dinner table. She is nursing a scotch. No one else seems to be around, which is strange because we are twenty minutes late.

"Where is everybody?" my father asks.

Joanne shrugs. Her usually effervescent voice is now almost a whisper.

"They're all out looking for Willy," she says.

"What do you mean?" my father asks.

"He must have jumped over the fence in the back," Joanne says. "I don't know how the hell he could have gotten over that fence, but he's not there. Maybe he jumped or slipped into the canal."

Willy is the half-shepherd, half-collie that Burt and his wife, Laurie, picked up as a pup from a farmer while they were hiding out in the country. He is almost full grown now, sixty or so pounds of awkward energy with a brain that has impressed no one but Burt, who calls him "my boy."

Joanne says they first noticed Willy was missing about an hour ago. Since then, Burt has been combing the neighborhood with Bill in one car, and Laurie has been driving alone in another.

The three of us sit silently, nibbling on some peanuts, perhaps more concerned that the festive evening we had looked forward to appears ruined than that Willie has disappeared.

"When is it ever going to end with him?" my father mutters. "When is the drama ever going to end?"

Perhaps twenty minutes pass and the door opens. Laurie walks in carrying Willy, who is soaking wet but seemingly all right. She lays him down on the living room rug and begins drying him off with towels. She had found him on a patch of mud near the end of the canal.

"He must have slipped off the dock and been unable to get back on," Laurie says. "Thank God the tide was out or he would have drowned."

Another fifteen minutes go by and Bill Miller and his son-in-law pull up. Bill, for most of his life a cop and undoubtedly one of the gentlest men to have ever donned a holster, walks in first.

He sees the dog, shakes his head and walks directly to the kitchen.

Burt, in jeans and an olive ski jacket, comes limping in behind Bill. He takes a step or two into the living room and stops. He sees the dog. He stands there frozen, only his head moving, eyes darting from person to person. Suddenly he breaks down, his voice a series of low moans turning into one long primal scream . . .

"Willy, Willy, Willy." The sound is so pure and so filled with anguish that it is both terrifying and cathartic.

The dog leaps from under the towels and is all over Burt, knocking him off balance, tail wagging, licking his face. Burt sinks to his knees. His eyes are wild. Tears are running down his cheeks. He is sobbing uncontrollably, violently.

Bill stays in the kitchen and begins carving the ham. Joanne keeps a tight grip on her scotch. My father's eyes are watery. Laurie walks up behind Burt and puts her arms around his neck.

I am confused.

Ten months earlier, on a warm Sunday afternoon in May of 1974, my phone rings. It is my brother and his voice is filled with the urgency I have come to expect as a political campaign draws to a close and he has some last-minute ideas he wants me to work on. I informally run the campaigns and am looked to for advice, but he calls the shots and does most of the work. As his brother, my major contribution is to get him to slow down.

On this day, I would like to bring him to a grinding halt. I have just come back from planting a garden at a friend's house in the country and I am covered with spring. On the way back, I stopped with my daughters to pick wild flowers. I am not feeling very political.

"Listen, Phil," he says. "I've got to talk to you."

"Let me guess. They just sent out a mailing calling you a child molester."

"C'mon, will you listen to me? Something incredible just happened. I think I was just paid a visit by the Mafia."

Good-bye spring.

"You were what?"

"Yeah, I'm sure of it. This guy I've never seen before comes to my apartment and says I've got to delay the board of adjustment vote on the Sutton property. He says that if the thing is voted down on Wednesday, a lot of lives are going to be ruined."

"What makes you think he's Mafia?"

"Everything. He was wearing a silk suit. He had on a big pinky ring. He was incredibly tough-looking. You know, big chest, broad shoulders, the works. I think I saw a gun under his jacket. And he wouldn't tell me his name. He called himself Joey D. He even turned up the volume on my TV set to make sure no one could listen to us. I'm telling you, it was like in the movies."

"What exactly did he want from you?"

"He kept saying that the vote has to be delayed for a few weeks because the banks are applying pressure and if it's voted down now, the whole thing will go under."

I ask my brother if that was the whole conversation. He says no. The guy who called himself Joey D. had said he could destroy the other slate in the upcoming primary, and he had asked Burt several times whether he had any money problems.

There are a number of thoughts racing through my head. They all come together in my next question.

"Burt, are you out of your goddamned head?"

He seems taken aback. "What do you mean?" he asks.

"What do I mean?" I shout. "What the hell is the matter with you? Some guy you don't know but think is Mafia comes to your apartment and asks if you have money problems. And you let him talk to you? Why didn't you say that if he didn't get out, you'd call the cops? That's what you should have done."

Burt answers in an exasperated voice that makes me feel like

4

a parent who has just told his teen-age daughter to be home before midnight.

"Aw, c'mon," he says. "I can take care of myself. If I had done what you said, that would have been the end of it. I'd never know who the guy was or whom he was representing or what kind of political information he had. I want to find out what the mystery is all about."

I'm beginning to think that my younger brother is more than just stubborn. He is an idiot.

"Look," I say, "this isn't some cops and robbers game you used to play. What's wrong with you? If you read this guy right, you're going to be in over your head. I'm telling you, these guys don't play games."

Burt remains silent for a few seconds. I hope that I have made an impression.

"Don't worry about a thing," he says finally. "Nothing happened that I can't take care of. And besides, I didn't give him the slightest indication that I would do anything. I even told him I couldn't do anything even if I wanted to. But he was very persistent. He just kept saying that people should be able to talk and help each other and that I should think about it. So I'll call the U.S. Attorney first thing in the morning and see what he says. And stop being so nervous. I know what I'm doing. I can live with myself."

There comes a point in all my conversations with my brother when he has heard everything he is going to hear and wants to get off the phone. We have now reached that point. I make one last try.

"Burt," I plead, "you're talking about living with yourself and I'm talking about living."

"Very funny," he says. "Send my love to the kids."

And so it begins.

Based on childhood appearance and intellect, Burt Ross was not a likely candidate to someday draw comparisons with Omar Sharif or to make the dean's list at Harvard. He didn't talk until he was past two. His ears stuck out so much that his parents considered taping them back. With one thumb in his mouth he liked to run the fingers of his free hand through other people's hair and contentedly repeat the words, "Golly, golly."

Even his name had a vaguely comic quality. When he was born, a nurse asked for the infant's full name. A middle name hadn't even been discussed, but his father suddenly felt compelled to provide his second child with a complete identity. "Burt Lee Ross," he blurted. Berkeley Industries was the company for which he worked.

At the time of his birth, Burt's parents had begun to achieve a measure of the financial security and middle-class respectability that were the guiding stars of so many first-generation Americans.

David Rosalsky—the name would become Ross when he was 27—was the youngest of seven children born to Lithuanian Jews who immigrated to New York in the 1880s and settled into tenement poverty. His father, who made his debut in the New World as a pushcart peddler, had severe epilepsy. The attacks would come with such sudden violence that David did not regret that his father left for work before he got up or that he returned late at night to eat alone and go to sleep. In thirty years the two exchanged barely a thousand words.

What familial benefits did accrue to David Rosalsky came largely from his being the youngest by eight years. Because most of his four brothers and two sisters had already left home while he was still a child, he got more than a full share of his mother's attention. And there was tangible fallout from the small businesses his brothers had opened. He had a second-hand bike. He was sent to camp for a summer. He went to Manual Training High School and had enough leisure time to become an accomplished runner and lacrosse player.

If, by the standards of his family, all this made him spoiled, it did not make him weak. The Red Hook section of Brooklyn he grew up in was Italian and rough. Jews defended themselves or were bullied. David chose to fight. He became so conditioned to protecting himself that once, when he was told someone had just beat up his kid brother, he belted the alleged perpetrator before remembering that he had no kid brother.

After Red Hook he went to college. Not just any college, but to the University of Virginia, which for a young man from the concrete jungle of New York seemed like four years in paradise. For most people those years meant the beginning of the Depression; for David Rosalsky, they were boom times. He was away from home, and he met people without his ghetto mentality. He was exposed to ideas that transcended reducing the inventory of a dry goods store. He was invited to estates in the rich clay countryside around Charlottesville, and he learned to ride a horse. Summers he worked as a busboy in the Catskills and bought a roadster with the money he saved. He fell in and out of love.

David Rosalsky came out of Virginia with the dream of becoming another Clarence Darrow. He started going to Brooklyn Law School but was soon summoned to a lower call-

7

ing: His brothers had started to manufacture razor blades, and they needed his help. The dream died, replaced by an unfulfilled fantasy that would haunt his nights in all the years to come.

By Labor Day weekend in 1937 he had been working for his brothers for a couple of years, was pulling in a nifty thirty-five dollars a week and needed a vacation. He went to Camp Tamiment, a singles resort in the Poconos. While waiting in line to take out a rowboat, he met the woman he would marry.

Her name was Rose Rogovin. She was a welfare department organizer and part-time teacher from the Bronx who had skipped a year in high school, majored in English at Hunter College and had begun studying for her masters at City College before dropping out to join the labor movement. She had both the bohemian and socialist aspirations that were common to her time. She hung out in Greenwich Village. She was amorously pursued by the poet Maxwell Bodenheim. She applauded the speakers who shouted the coming of a just society.

David Rosalsky was none of these things, but there was something about him that made her feel he was the one. He was passionate in nonpolitical ways. When she leaned on him, he didn't bend. Most of the other men in her life were drifters; he seemed to know where he was going. And even though the direction he was headed in had not been part of her conscious itinerary, that he knew what he wanted was in itself reassuring.

Rose Rogovin still lived with her parents and younger brother and sister, and Dave Rosalsky quickly adopted her family as his own. Her father was a Polish immigrant who had a keen intellect and a good education but had been forced to earn an unhappy living auctioning off the wares of bankrupt stores. Dave Rosalsky listened to her father speak in a Yiddish that was literary compared with that spoken in his own home. He learned from him about Zionism. But most of all, he began to understand the quality of giving. Louis Rogovin was a man who sneaked extra money to people whose wares he had just auctioned off because he couldn't stand profiting from other people's misery. He brought strangers in off the street for a warm meal. He refused to eat sugar during the war because there was a shortage and he thought the soldiers needed it. He sometimes displayed a violent temper with his children, but he cried when the Allies bombed Berlin.

Rose's mother was a simple woman with twinkling eyes who sometimes laughed so hard she wet her pants. Dave Rosalsky naturally came to call her "Mom." He loved her cooking. He helped her son get a job. He played ping pong with her younger daughter. The whole family was crazy about him.

The courtship was brief. They were married on Lincoln's Birthday in 1938 and settled into a small apartment across the street from Yankee Stadium. Rose taught until the birth of her first son a year and a half later. Dave continued working for his brothers and changed his name to Ross because they had changed theirs. His salary continued to grow and by 1943, when Burt was born, the family was living in a rented home in Teaneck, New Jersey, a model suburban town five miles west of the George Washington Bridge and Fort Lee.

Berkeley Industries continued to prosper through the war, and by 1948 David Ross was making nearly $30,000 a year. Then he did a rather gutsy thing for a man with a family and a mortgage on his home. He quit. For years he had been promised a partnership by his brother-in-law, but nothing ever materialized. So with three other men and a total investment of $14,000, he opened a factory in Newark that first manufactured folding rules and then steel measuring tapes. His wife went back to teaching. He worked seven days a week and did his share of the physical labor. In the clichéd tradition of American success stories, it paid off. By 1950 the company was beginning to see daylight. Ten years later Evans Rule went public and David Ross, at forty-nine, was a wealthy man.

The year 1950 should have been a good one for David and Rose Ross—but it wasn't. In September, seven-year-old Burt

9

became ill with what seemed to be the flu. But when the nausea, fever and aching bones disappeared, he was left with one other symptom. He couldn't walk.

The diagnosis was polio. The recommended treatment for his paralyzed right leg was six months at the Sister Kenney Institute in Jersey City. The prognosis was for a life on crutches or, with a little luck, a knee brace. Ironically, the night before Burt became sick, his father had coached him in starting positions for a track meet he was to have been in the next day. Burt had shown signs that he was going to be a hell of an athlete. And he loved competition.

Parts of a personality began to emerge over the next year. When other children cried after visiting hours at the hospital, a nurse would wheel Burt over to cheer them up. Others screamed when hot wax was applied to their afflicted limbs. Burt didn't. Most kids would mope away the long days. Burt organized wheelchair races in the halls.

He was discharged just before his eighth birthday and he had done well enough to go directly into a brace. The day he was fitted began anxiously for his parents. Would their son's brace be an emotional stigma? The answer came moments after they left the orthopedic supply store. Burt approached the first passerby, lifted his pants leg and with apparent pride raised his brace for the man to see. It was to be like this for years to come. If anyone happened to miss the fact that he was lame, Burt made sure they found out. And if all this bravado meant was that his leg was only a weakness if others discovered it on their own, there may have been worse ways of coping with a handicap.

Burt came home from the hospital at an age when for most boys athletic ability and status are synonymous. He refused to go to the rear of the line. Instead, he pursued the very sports which required two good legs. Baseball was his favorite, and he managed to play by using a pinch runner and fielding first base. In races at elementary school he would figure out the handicap he needed to make himself competitive, then limp eagerly toward the finish line. The only vocal expression he gave to his inner pain came years later in a softball game. He had hit a long drive over the left fielder's head. As he dove headfirst for second base, a friend almost tagged him out. "You know," Burt said, a look of hurt in his eyes as he picked himself up, "for anyone else that would have been a homer."

Over the next five years, Burt's walking improved more than anyone, with the exception of Burt, had anticipated. His mother devoted herself to watching him exercise, getting him the best physical therapists and searching the country for top orthopedic specialists. When one of them told her that his walking would probably not improve much Burt looked directly at the doctor and asked angrily, "Who do you think you are, God?" At thirteen he underwent the first of two corrective operations. Just before the anesthesiologist clamped the mask over him, Burt broke up the surgeon by shouting, "Okay, butchers, hack away." Two years later he was able to discard the brace. By the time he entered college, when he walked slowly there was barely a trace of a limp.

As his leg continued to improve, it ceased to be the primary focus of his parents' attention. Some of the other things they began noticing about him were mildly disturbing. Burt generally seemed cynical about events around him. When he insisted that the big television quiz shows in the mid-fifties were fixed, his father yelled, "What the hell do you believe in?"

Burt got his gleeful vindication on that one, but on a more important matter there was little laughter. Burt didn't have friends. There were kids he played with, but he seemed more intent on beating them at something than in sharing anything intimate. At first his parents assumed he was trying to compensate for his leg and would change as he got older. Then they began to remember incidents that predated his illness. One of those memories was of a five-year-old who used to throw his paddle across the room in rage when he lost a ping-pong game.

Burt himself showed a painful awareness of his friendless condition. When he was fourteen, he began ninth grade at the George School, a coed Quaker boarding school in Bucks County, Pennsylvania. He was elected president of his class, which his parents took as a sign that he was loosening up. "Sorry," he corrected them, "but that's not the way it is. I don't kid myself. No one voted for me because they like me. They just knew that I would do the best job."

That election was the first real indication that Burt had any interest in government, or at least in politics and power. He was reelected the following year and would probably have been a four-term president had it not been for his health. He returned home after his sophomore year in such an exhausted state, his five-foot, eight-inch frame reduced to 125 pounds, that he had to spend most of the summer recuperating, and his mother forced him to cut back on his activities.

Work was what seemed to keep him going. He became editor in chief of the school newspaper, organized a boycott against a local barbershop that wouldn't serve blacks and studied so hard that an elderly French teacher confided in his parents: "Burt didn't really deserve an A, but I would have felt guilty giving him anything less. I've just never seen anyone work as much."

The barbershop boycott demonstrated another growing part of Burt's personality that some people viewed with alarm. Abrasiveness. When he spoke to school authorities about his plan, they suggested that the power of friendly persuasion be tried instead. Burt would have none of it. There was nothing to be friendly about, he said. Wrong was wrong. So he went ahead and launched his boycott. When it proved successful and the barbershop changed its policy, Burt was convinced his approach had been right. Others remained skeptical. "Burt's values are all in the right place," a teacher suggested to his parents, "but I think he could benefit by learning that honesty and tact are not mutually exclusive."

If tact was not to be Burt's strong suit, neither was modesty.

During his senior year at George School he was invited to appear with other high school editors on the nationally telecast "Dorothy Gordon Youth Forum." The day of the show, his family expressed concern that he was not well prepared.

"Why is it that I'm the only one who's not nervous?" Burt asked. "I'm the one who's going on the show and you better learn to relax. I promise you, this won't be the only time in my life that I'll be on television."

He did well on that show and well enough in school to get into Harvard, an achievement his parents viewed with mixed emotions. They were proud of his success, but they feared that hard work alone would not get him by in the company of geniuses. And they continued to worry about a son who did so well but seemed to enjoy it so little.

"Make some friends at Harvard," his mother counseled.

"Do you think anyone ever said that to Franklin Roosevelt?" he answered.

"Have a little fun this summer," his father suggested as Burt left on a youth tour of Europe before he began college. "You're eighteen and the women there are more sophisticated about sex. Have a few experiences. Enjoy yourself."

"You can stop worrying" were the only words on the first postcard Burt sent home.

His parents' concern that work alone wouldn't cut it at Harvard seemed justified after they received his first midterm report. He was in danger of failing two subjects.

"Don't worry," he reassured them. "I'm just getting a feel of the way things work here. I'll take care of everything."

He made the dean's list his last three years, and in what may have been a rare happening among Jewish families, he increasingly showed that he was smarter than his parents thought.

Academic matters were by no means foremost on Burt's agenda. Any lingering doubts about his love for politics disappeared by his sophomore year. He joined the Harvard-Radcliffe Young Democratic Club and quickly was elected to its thirteen-member executive committee. At the time the Club had fewer than two hundred members and a program that was something less than vital.

Burt wasted no time in changing that. The Club's president had invited George Wallace to speak and Burt seized the opportunity to sign up new members. By knocking on undergraduates' doors and explaining that for little more than the cost of hearing Wallace as a nonmember they could join the Club and hear other speakers as well, he soon doubled the membership.

But as word of Wallace's upcoming appearance spread around campus, opposition grew. The Harvard Crimson editorialized against the invitation. The Harvard Law School's Democratic Club disassociated itself from the event. And the African-Asian Society, whose members included Burt's Ugandan roommate, passed a resolution condemning Wallace's appearance.

The president of the Club got cold feet. First he said the event should be rearranged as a debate. When Wallace refused, he decided the invitation should be withdrawn. Burt was furious. He argued that the invitation in no way represented an endorsement of Wallace, that the other speakers scheduled throughout the year were liberals and that students were smart enough to see through a demagogue, if that's what Wallace was. Most important, he shouted, he had just sold two hundred memberships based on Wallace's coming. To cancel the date now would make him guilty of misrepresentation.

To no avail. The president announced that if the executive committee didn't back him, he would resign. Now Burt saw more than an issue involved. He lobbied his way to a 7–6 victory in the controversy, and when the president resigned, Burt offered himself as a candidate to replace him. Using car pools to get out his vote on the night of the election, he picked up his margin of victory from the very students he had recently signed up for the Wallace speech.

Elected in controversy, Burt did nothing to dispel the image.

14

The Club's membership quintupled during his two years as president. Speakers he attracted to the campus included Martin Luther King, Senators McGovern and Muskie, Richard Daley, Adam Clayton Powell and Roy Wilkens. But the Harvard Crimson, whose top editors were friends of the president Burt had replaced, decided that he ran the Club as his personal fiefdom. It attacked him frequently as "Boss Ross."

Burt himself conceded that he wasn't too keen on parliamentary procedures. It seemed to him that if he did most of the work, he should have most of the say. He also grew impatient with endless discussions that to him signified nothing. He wanted action.

Toward friends Burt showed great loyalty. For instance he had found it difficult to get a faculty member willing to introduce Wallace until a professor of government stepped forward. A few months later, when Burt heard Martin Luther King was coming, he reached for the phone and called the same man.

"Dr. King is coming and I think you ought to introduce him," Burt said. "You've earned it."

Toward enemies Burt was not one to turn the other cheek. When King arrived on campus and was deluged by the media, Burt noticed a Crimson reporter start to ask a question.

"I'm sorry," Burt said, putting his arm around King's shoulder and turning him away from the reporter, "but if you guys don't play ball with me, I don't play ball with you. There will be no interview with Dr. King."

Inside the ivied walls of academia a politician was learning his craft. At times, Burt at Harvard seemed as likely as Fanny Foxe on a pulpit. His north-Jersey accent made him sound like a truck driver. And there was nothing cosmopolitan about his ways. On being introduced to Princess Christina of Sweden, who was studying at Radcliffe, Burt said: "I'm delighted to meet you. I've heard that Copenhagen is one of the most beautiful cities in the world."

At the same time, he demonstrated a capacity to relate very

effectively to royalty of a different kind. After spending the summer between his freshman and sophomore years working for a New Jersey congressman, Burt decided he was ready to step up in class. He applied for a summer job with Senator Ted Kennedy. During his interview with Kennedy's legislative assistant, Burt didn't talk about idealism. The real reason he should be hired, he suggested, was that the Harvard-Radcliffe Young Democrats hadn't endorsed Kennedy in a previous Democratic primary fight. While the lack of endorsement hadn't affected the election, Burt reasoned, it must have stung the Senator's pride to be rejected by his alma mater. Burt made it clear that he could offer the Club's active support in the future. Hundreds of other applicants put forth their credentials. Burt offered a deal. Kennedy personally called to welcome him aboard.

Politics took up most but not all of Burt's spare time. He did volunteer work teaching chess, journalism and public speaking at a local prison. And he had his first passionate relationship with a girl.

He had met her during the summer, but because she went to school in Pennsylvania, it was largely a love affair by mail. There was one odd aspect to their correspondence. Burt kept copies of all the letters he wrote her. After a year she broke off with him, suggesting in her "Dear Burt" letter that he wasn't spontaneous enough. Someone suggested to him that the copies of his letters might be a symptom of what she was talking about.

"But if she refers to something I wrote," Burt asked, "how can I be sure that was what I said unless I have my letter to refer to?"

If easygoing relationships with other people were not his greatest strength, there was plenty of spontaneity in other areas of his life. In fact, Burt began to develop a small reputation for his feats of derring-do. On several occasions, when he spotted a drunk driver weaving around, Burt would force the drunk's car to the side of the road and grab the keys from the startled occupant.

"You could get killed doing that," a cop to whom Burt had given the keys after one such rundown advised him.

"Yeah, but how could I live with myself if I picked up the paper the next day and read that the guy had jumped a curb and killed a kid?" Burt replied.

He spent the summer between his junior and senior years working in his father's factory and soon became obsessed with security measures there he was sure were too lax. His father told him not to worry about it. Undeterred, Burt drove alone to the factory one night, squeezed himself through a partially open window and loaded up his trunk with hundreds of dollars in merchandise. Then he drove to his parents' apartment, deposited his heist in front of their door and rang the bell.

"That," said Burt, triumphantly showing the evidence to his bewildered father, "is how good your damn security is."

Throughout his years at Harvard it became apparent that Burt was most comfortable when he was performing publicly in a one-man show. Addressing audiences of a thousand or more he seemed totally relaxed. He could be funny, warm, even intimate. But sitting in a room with a few people who wanted to talk about movies, sex or personal problems, Burt came off as edgy, inhibited and awkward. His conversation was heavy, his humor forced. He always had one eye on the door.

Equally clear was that Burt envied others their close friendships. To compensate for what he couldn't find in his present, he attempted to resurrect his past. He made frequent visits to George School, to the camp he had gone to, to the few elementary school playmates with whom he had maintained contact. Nor was his nostalgia limited to people and places. It included things, especially his own. Burt refused to throw anything away. Over the years he accumulated cartons of report cards, letters, class notes and photographs. He joked that they would all be donated someday to the library that would be built in his honor. Part of him may have believed that. Part of him also needed the comfort that he could only find in his memory.

The six years following his graduation from Harvard were all downhill. Burt had decided to go to law school, the natural next step toward a good living and a career in politics. He assumed he would go to Harvard, Yale or Columbia. His law boards put him in the 90th percentile, but that wasn't quite good enough. He was rejected by all three. It was the first real defeat of his life, and he was crushed. He began to come apart.

He enrolled at the University of Pennsylvania Law School, a good school but less prestigious. He hated Philadelphia and after a year, transferred to New York University to finish up. During his last year he decided that he didn't want to practice criminal law after all. "What it boils down to," he said, "is that I'd be spending most of my time defending crooks."

Still, he unenthusiastically got his degree and passed the bar exam, all the while preparing to go into his father's business. He would make a good living and he would start at the top, a position he hadn't enjoyed for three years. Then that option, too, was suddenly unavailable to him. His father decided to retire and since Evans Rule was already publicly held, the welcome mat was taken in.

Until Burt left Harvard, politics had been his obsession. Now it became money. He wanted lots of it and he wanted it fast. He couldn't say why or how much, only that when he earned enough maybe he'd take a year or two off and travel around the world.

So he became a stockbroker, and tapping every business associate and golf crony his father ever had, Burt did begin to make good money. Nearly $40,000 his first year. In the same way he had saved his childhood allowance while other kids were spending theirs on baseball cards, now he saved his commissions. He said he wanted to invest in real estate. The truth was that he no longer knew what he wanted. His self-confidence was eroding.

18

He was losing all sense of direction.

He rented an apartment in Manhattan, and since his ears had grown in without taping and his soft brown eyes and swarthy good looks commanded considerable attention, he had little trouble arranging one-night stands.

The one active tie he maintained with his past involved interviewing prospective Harvard students from the New York region. Yet when he applied for membership to the Harvard Club in Manhattan, he was rejected.

"Do you believe in contributing financially to the University?" one of his interviewers asked him.

Burt, who was the biggest Harvard donor in his class, and was being sponsored by a man who headed alumni giving, decided the whole process was idiotic. "No," he said.

"Do you want to join the Club for business reasons or pleasure?" someone else asked him. Burt, who wanted to learn to play squash, said it was purely a business decision.

"Well, I don't think I should write that down," the man said.

"Then why did you ask me the question?" Burt asked.

The admissions committee decided that he should submit to another round of interviews. Burt withdrew his application and drew deeper into his shell. He began spending more time with his parents, who by now had moved from Teaneck to a penthouse in Fort Lee. He returned frequently to his old schools.

At his graduation from Harvard, Burt had been given a plaque with an inscription that read: "Burt Ross has been the dynamic, controversial and extraordinarily successful president of the Harvard–Radcliffe Young Democrats. There is probably no student in the present senior class who has the same combination of both drive and natural aptitude for the political life. One thing is certain. His career will be well worth watching."

If anyone happened to be watching in late spring of 1971, he would have seen a twenty-eight-year-old who had nothing to show. Burt Lee Ross's youth was slipping away. He was restless. He was frightened.

3

Burt Lee Ross was named after a razor blade company. Fort Lee, New Jersey did even worse. General Charles Lee, the man George Washington chose to honor with a fort, turned out to be a traitor.

General Washington had the small fort built in 1776, shortly after the signing of the Declaration of Independence. Fort Lee was supposed to be a depot for troops in case reinforcements were needed for the defense of Fort Washington, which was directly across the Hudson River in Manhattan. But less than a month after Fort Lee was finished, Fort Washington was overrun by General Cornwallis's British army and the New Jersey fort became the starting point of one of the great retreats in military history as Washington led his routed troops south to the Delaware River.

It was not to be the only retreat from Fort Lee. In 1840, there were only thirty dwellings spread out atop the majestic Palisades, rising 250 feet from the Hudson River to the two and one-half square miles that are now Fort Lee. Fifty years later, the population had swelled to 1,600, a steam railroad and trolley line were built and the town had become a thriving resort area. It didn't last long. When Palisades Amusement Park opened on

Fort Lee's southern border in 1897, the honky-tonk mood soon had the wealthy guests at the exclusive hotels going elsewhere.

On March 29, 1904, thirty-nine years to the day before Burt Ross was born, Fort Lee was incorporated as a borough. The town celebrated by playing host to America's newest industry: the movies. From 1905 to 1915, Fort Lee was where films were made. Universal, Peerless, Vitagraph and Essanay built their studios there. Passengers on the 125th Street ferry from New York included Mary Pickford, Douglas Fairbanks, Charlie Chaplin, Theda Bara, D. W. Griffith, Lillian Gish and Buster Keaton. The Barrymores actually lived in Fort Lee. Hoot Gibson and Will Rogers twirled their lassos on the cliffs. Pearl White dangled from the Palisades in "The Perils of Pauline." Some of the locals were making more than a hundred dollars a week. The future looked bright.

But Fort Lee had problems. The ferry trip was time-consuming. Uncertain weather cut into outdoor shooting schedules. And the cost of heating the indoor sets in the huge studios was enormous. In 1913 Sam Goldwyn, Jessie Lasky and Cecil B. DeMille decided to make a film called "The Squaw Man" and went west to scout for a location. The place they found was Hollywood.

By the late twenties, the population had leveled off at 8,000 and the town was going nowhere. But as construction of the George Washington Bridge began, a new wave of optimism swept the community. The Jersey side of the bridge would empty into the heart of Fort Lee. Everyone thought a boom was on the way. What was on the way was the Depression. The bridge opened in 1931; two years later the town went bankrupt.

In 1940 only 9,400 people lived in Fort Lee, and in 1950 there were barely 2,000 more. Even in the postwar period of economic prosperity and suburban expansion, Fort Lee remained the retarded child. New Yorkers stopped there to get gas and a road map, then drove on to buy homes in more affluent Bergen County towns like Teaneck and Englewood. Instead of the gateway to New Jersey, Fort Lee had become a place to get away from.

By the thirties the town was largely Italian. The few newcomers were Italian as well. Some of them were also Mafia. First came the Mustache Petes, the old-fashioned, first-generation mobsters who wanted to conduct their business in New York and raise their children in flower gardens. Then came the Young Turks, names that would spawn legends. Albert Anastasia, who headed what was known as Murder, Inc. and was himself launched into eternity from a barber chair, bought an estate in town and surrounded it with watchdogs. Joseph Doto, better known as Joe Adonis, was a chief in Frank Costello's gambling combine and helped turn Bergen County into the Las Vegas of the east. Adonis was finally deported to Italy, but when he died in 1971 his mortal remains were returned to Fort Lee, where they now rest in Madonna Cemetery. "Tony Bender" Strollo, a hit man for Vito Genovese, lived in town until he himself was hit. Tommy Ryan Eboli was a fight manager who lost his license after attacking a referee. He started working as Anastasia's chauffeur and eventually rose to such heights that he, too, qualified for summary execution.

The ones who didn't live or die in Fort Lee came to eat and meet there. Yet with the exception of gambling, the town was not heavily worked. Gambling was no small exception, however. The Kefauver Senate investigating committee of 1950 spotlighted Fort Lee as a town in which housewives were building nest eggs by using their telephones to relay betting information. Limousines nightly carried sporting gentlemen from New York to lay their wagers at the Riviera, a classy night spot that hugged the Palisades. One policeman was said to have run his own game in a barn. A police chief was found with a bullet in his head. The death was ruled a suicide, although some people found it hard to understand how he could have shot himself, died instantly and then thrown the weapon to where it was found, several yards away.

So from a nothing town, Fort Lee in the forties and early fifties became an unsavory one. The Mafia image was to hold even as the big names passed from the scene. By 1975 the Fort Lee cast of "wise guys," as cops call them, had dwindled to a small bunch of no-names. When Anthony "Tony C" Carminati was arrested for loan-sharking in May of 1975, the police called him one of Jersey's biggest organized crime figures, yet barely anyone had ever heard of him. Luciano, Costello, Lansky: everyone knew about them. But the names of latter-day Fort Lee residents with mob ties would ring no bells. Adonis's son, Joe Doto, Jr., still lived in town, but he was more a splinter than a chip off the old block. When he was arrested in 1974 for bank robbery, some people thought they heard his father turn in the grave.

By the mid-fifties Fort Lee, underpopulated and strategically located, was like a plump chicken strutting its feathers and waiting to be plucked. Finally the axe fell. Developers began buying up land and a Republican administration that had been entrenched as long as anyone could remember soon rezoned property for high-rise apartment buildings.

The head of Fort Lee's Republican Party until his death in 1970 was J. Fletcher Creamer, Sr. Creamer's real estate companies owned millions of dollars of land and buildings in town, and his construction company did a considerable amount of work for the borough.

Creamer's political lieutenant and real estate partner was Edward McDermott, whose father had been a Fort Lee police chief in the forties. McDermott was employed full time as tax collector. His salary was $15,400 a year. The assessed value of his real estate holdings in town exceeded $4 million.

Fort Lee's Mayor in the sixties was Joseph Licata. In 1971, amid reports of federal investigations into Fort Lee, the former bandleader decided not to seek a third term. He said he had a stomach ailment. When he left office, Licata's family had almost a million dollars in local real estate holdings.

The first of Fort Lee's high-rise apartments, Horizon House, opened in 1962. By 1971 nearly twenty more had followed. The population was officially listed at 31,000, but people were moving in so fast that a truer figure was probably 35,000. Into these luxury buildings came people like Dave and Rose Ross, who had raised their children in homes and no longer wanted the responsibility of ownership. There were also large numbers of young couples who were not yet ready to buy their first home, and a variety of other upper-middle-class types who liked apartment living but were afraid to remain in New York.

In ten years, Fort Lee went through the kinds of changes that took other towns half a century. From a sleepy, rural community it became what many called the "sixth borough of New York." By 1971 more than half the residents lived in apartments. Six major highways converged at the George Washington Bridge. The streets were jammed. The shopping facilities were inadequate. The schools were overcrowded. Esthetically the town looked like it had been planned by a kindergarten fingerpainting class.

There was one other thing. No one seemed to like anyone else. The old-time Italian and Greek homeowners resented the wealthy Jewish tenants who moved into the big buildings which were destroying their sleepy neighborhoods. And they were angry that despite the additional tax revenues the apartments generated, their taxes had still tripled in ten years.

The tenants hated landlords who could double their rent at lease end. And they, too, felt closed in by all the new building. The trauma of rapid change and ugly growth had resulted in an undercurrent of helpless anger.

By the spring of 1971, Fort Lee was drifting. And so was Burt Lee Ross.

4

In June of 1971 Burt was asked by a wealthy client to give a fund-raising party in his parents' penthouse for Birch Bayh. The senator from Indiana was going nowhere in his quest for the Democratic presidential nomination, and Burt personally preferred McGovern. Still, he agreed. He didn't want to say no to a big investor. He had an affinity for national figures, and however irrelevant, this would be his first political activity since he got out of college.

Soon after the party was announced Burt got a call from Ted Hanser, a serious young man who said he'd like to meet Bayh but couldn't afford the $50 tab. Burt told him to come anyway. Then, almost as an afterthought, Hanser mentioned that he was a local Democratic committeeman. The man the Democrats had recently nominated to run for mayor, he said, was moving to the Midwest. Might Burt be interested in taking his place? He wouldn't have to give up his job, Hanser said encouragingly. Being mayor was only a part-time position.

Burt didn't know much about Fort Lee politics, but he did know that Democrats there didn't win elections. Indeed, a stranger asking him if he wanted to run for mayor seemed a good indication of how desperate they were. But if the Democrats had nothing going, neither did Burt. He said he'd be happy to talk about it.

They met. Hanser explained that since the Democratic candidate had stepped down after the primary, it was now up to the party's forty committee members to pick a successor. Eight members had been chosen to interview candidates and make recommendations to the entire committee. Some people were pushing Abe Safro, a middle-aged dentist who had run unsuccessfully for council a few years back, but the nomination still seemed up for grabs. Hanser suggested that Burt meet with Len Kramer, who was on the nominating committee and wasn't crazy about Safro.

Kramer, a bald, square-jawed old-timer, was a man of strong convictions. The two met in Kramer's modest garden apartment. The political analysis Kramer offered made Burt feel like he was contending for the privilege of committing suicide. By the mid-sixties, he said, the Democrats had begun inching into Republican majorities. But in 1968 the regular organization had endorsed Johnson for reelection, a splinter group had backed McCarthy, and the party went to war with itself. Three years later a lot of people still weren't talking to each other.

With Kramer's encouraging analysis and support, Burt went before the nominating committee. Max Lazarus, one of two candidates for the council, ushered Burt to his back porch. His running mate, Mike Mosolino, was already there. Both men were in their early forties and like the others in the room, stonefaced.

Burt had not been told what to expect. His bell-bottom pants and flowered shirt seemed out of place in a room full of gray slacks and receding hairlines. He had the distinct feeling that his drooping moustache was in itself a major barrier.

Someone asked about his political experience and he had to fall back on college. As he talked, it occurred to him that Harvard was being received on the same wavelength as Peking. He told them he was a stockbroker, then realized he was not among investors. In the end, he could not say anything that bore the slightest relationship to Fort Lee.

When Burt stammered to a halt, Pete McGuire, a small man with an elfin expression, began. He spoke in a slow, heavy brogue.

"And how old are you?" McGuire asked.

"Twenty-eight," Burt said.

"Well, what I want to be askin' is what makes you think a young whippersnapper like yourself without any experience whatsoever is ready to step right into the big leagues?"

Burt swallowed the laugh that had begun to rise in his throat. He paused briefly, balancing his natural belligerence against his self-interest. Then the scale tipped and he answered with an uneasy smile.

"Mr. McGuire," he said, "if I were the manager of a team that had been losing games for thirty years, I'd be willing to try anything."

That was that. A few more voices asked strained questions and Burt was shown out. Kramer called him later that night. The committee had voted seven to one against him.

"You have to be out of your mind to want to be Mayor of Fort Lee," Burt's mother comforted him. "This is the best thing that could have happened to you."

"We ought to celebrate," his father said. "Go have a nice vacation."

But Kramer, who had prevented the shutout, said it wasn't over yet. The nominating committee's recommendation was nonbinding. Maybe Burt could round up some support before the entire committee voted next week.

Burt had no one to take on vacation, and the thought of being unable to get something that hardly anyone else wanted intensified his sense of failure. So he began making phone calls and setting up meetings with small cliques of committee members.

To his surprise, some of these people were young and a few seemed liberal. Several even expressed enthusiasm about making him the sacrificial lamb.

One of these committeemen was Roy Sampath, a squat East Indian with long, stringy hair and a boil on his nose that Burt at first mistook for a religious ornament. Sampath had led the McCarthy insurgents in 1968 and had briefly ruled the Democratic Party in Fort Lee. He was liberal and articulate. But he was such a controversial political figure that his tenure as party chief did not last for long.

Now Sampath seized on Burt as his ticket back to power. He talked Burt up to his remaining followers, and Burt let him. Burt complimented Sampath on his intelligence. He nodded in agreement when Sampath launched into a political diatribe punctuated with "counterproductives" and "I submits."

The Democrats convened to choose a mayoral candidate on a muggy night in late July. They met in an elementary school auditorium, and as Burt walked in, he did a quick head count. Only twenty-eight of the forty committee members had shown.

Someone Burt did not recognize nominated Safro. Hanser nominated Burt. The room grew quiet. No other names were being put forth.

Safro was called to the platform first. In confident, almost pious tones he droned on about his service to the community, his dedication to the party, his knowledge of Fort Lee. Burt was seeing Safro for the first time. He reminded him of a rabbi.

Then it was Burt's turn. Although the audience was too small for him to relax fully, he spoke concisely and well. The Democrats could win this year, he said, but it would take the right man and the right campaign to do it. His lack of experience in Fort Lee, he suggested, was a plus. He had no enemies. He could work with everyone. He would wage an aggressive campaign.

Safro had offered them himself. Burt had promised them a winner. The two were asked to leave the room. They waited at opposite ends of the corridor. Twenty minutes later the auditorium doors opened. Burt had gotten eighteen votes. The brass ring was his.

Ordinarily one begins a local political campaign by mapping out the issues. Burt began by buying a map of Fort Lee. That he didn't even live in town put him at a distinct disadvantage. He quickly moved in with his parents, but it was still weeks before he could drive to campaign headquarters without getting lost.

When he finally arrived, he found nothing encouraging. The headquarters was a dilapidated storefront squeezed between a pizza shop and a beauty parlor in a run-down section of Main Street. Someone put some fresh paint on the walls, but it didn't help much. The back door had been ripped off. The fan didn't work. The leg of Burt's desk kept collapsing.

One of two old schoolmates Burt convinced to work for him was doing a brilliant job organizing a card file that no one but he understood. The other, whom Burt had bought a suit and taken to the barber, was on the phone telling girl friends that politics was "a heavy trip." A fat man in his thirties came in every night to describe his latest triumph at the local singles club. A woman known as Drunken Mary teetered by regularly to ask where the Governor was. A young man with cerebral palsy wanted to discuss Greek mythology. And Roy Sampath, who was on the roof installing lights for a sign, refused to come inside because of his differences with Max Lazarus and Mike Mosolino, Burt's running mates.

By the third week in August, Burt was coming home from work early and ringing doorbells until after dark. He had learned that the town was divided about evenly between home-owners and tenants. The Italian and Greek homeowners had always voted overwhelmingly Republican. The predominantly Jewish tenants for the most part didn't vote. The line on them was that in their self-enclosed luxury buildings with their swim-

29

ming pools and views of the Manhattan skyline, tenants thought their governor was Rockefeller.

Burt settled on a simple strategy. He reasoned that since tenants would vote Democratic if they could be convinced to vote, he would hold back on them until the end of the campaign. For now he would concentrate on enemy territory.

Each night Burt walked through block after block of rectangular brick homes. He would exchange a few words at each door, then put a check mark next to the names of those people who had seemed friendly. In the beginning, there weren't many check marks.

Ellen Levine was one of the young women who frequently accompanied Burt on his walking tours. She was a bright and good-looking magazine editor who had gone to Wellesley and had known Burt for years. His brassiness appealed to her. When he called her, it was not so much to ask for her help as to demand it.

"How did I do?" he asked her after their first evening of bell ringing.

"You talk too much," Ellen said.

It was advice that only began to sink in a few weeks later, when a man Burt spent an hour convincing to vote Democratic turned out to be from another town.

When Burt finally started listening to people, he couldn't believe what he sometimes heard.

"I'm fed up with the Democrats who are running this town," one man shouted at him.

"Excuse me," Burt said, "but the Democrats haven't controlled Fort Lee in thirty years."

"Don't you try to fool me, young fellow," the man snorted before slamming his door in Burt's face.

Burt's troubles were by no means confined to strangers. By early September his vows to bring peace to the party had been broken. He had counted heavily on getting large numbers of new tenants to register to vote. To accomplish this, he wanted to set up registration tables every night in apartment lobbies and shopping centers. Len Kramer and his wife, who were in charge of the registration drive, thought that a few evenings in some churches would be sufficient. Burt made what for him was a major effort to be diplomatic. When that didn't work, he exploded. The Kramers quit the drive. Sampath succeeded them; still, there were no results. Again Burt blew up; now he had lost his original sponsors. The list of Ross haters was beginning to grow.

Even when Burt took charge of the registration drive himself the results were mixed. One evening a peripatetic friend of his from Manhattan hitchhiked across the George Washington Bridge to help register voters in high rise apartments. The first bell Don Reilly rang was answered by a man wearing a red silk bathrobe. This threw Don back a little. He was unaccustomed to a community where people retired for the night before Walter Cronkite had signed off.

Reilly asked tentatively whether the man was registered to vote. He said no. When Reilly asked if he would like to register, the man said yes. Encouraged, Reilly informed him that he could register at that very moment in his own lobby. The man said he was sorry, but it wasn't convenient right now. Reilly was perplexed.

"Since the registration table will only be here tonight," he said, "I can't imagine that it will ever be more convenient for you."

"As a matter of fact," the man said, "it will never be less convenient."

Reilly must have looked bewildered because the man invited him in for an explanation. He led him through his living room to a door, and without saying anything, opened it. Inside was his bedroom and on the bed were two nude women.

"Now do you understand why it's inconvenient?" the man asked.

"I certainly do," Reilly said and beat a hasty exit.

In every successful uphill campaign there comes a turning point, an event which in retrospect caused the momentum to turn around. For Burt, that point came in mid-September. Until then his big issue had been a cable-TV franchise which he believed the mayor and council had improperly awarded. It was an issue that was putting people to sleep.

"We've got to forget the cable thing," he announced after returning to headquarters late one night. "Nobody gives a damn about it. I've been ringing doorbells for a month now and I think I've figured out what's on people's minds. Homeowners care about their taxes. Tenants care about their rents. And everybody is against all the high-rise apartment construction."

Within days, a slogan was hatched: "High Rises, High Taxes, High Rents. High Time For A Change." The expression "concrete jungle" became the catchword of the campaign. A moratorium on high-rise construction was incorporated as the key plank in the Democratic platform.

As issues began to take hold, so did Burt's tremendous energy. Young couples began volunteering to canvass apartment buildings, make phone calls and put up posters. Friends of the Rosses joined regular party workers and helped stuff envelopes. High school kids spent their weekends delivering campaign literature in exchange for pizza and cokes. Headquarters came to life.

Burt's own drive was responsible for much of the growing enthusiasm, but the Republicans' ineptitude didn't hurt any. The only issue they were scoring any points on was Burt's residency. They walked around town with a Manhattan phone book opened to his name and Central Park West address. He was a carpetbagger, they sneered. Pressed for an answer, Burt hedged. He said the Manhattan apartment was rented only as a convenience to out-of-town business clients.

The man the Republicans had selected to succeed Mayor Joe Licata was Myril Neiman, president of the six-man council. Neiman was a soft-spoken, decent man who had lived in town all his life. Political shrewdness, however, was not his greatest talent. When Burt charged that the Republican council had voted unanimously on the last thousand roll calls, Neiman replied, "We disagree in private but we vote together at meetings because we think it looks better for the public."

When Burt suggested to his running mates that the Republican candidates might be less than heavyweights, they remained skeptical.

"Don't feel too confident," Max said. "They'll drop a bomb on us before the campaign is over. They always do."

Burt continued to campaign eight hours a day, twelve on weekends. He developed a coterie of attractive women who wore straw hats and gave away balloons as they accompanied him through shopping centers. He waited at bus stops to shake hands with commuters. He reached into swimming pools and visited tennis courts to hustle votes.

In addition to all his public campaigning, Burt engaged in a little private intrigue. One of the Republican councilmen was Harvey Salb, a dentist who looked a little like Art Buchwald. Burt had heard rumors that Salb was upset with his party because he had been bypassed for Neiman. He figured that if he could get Salb to endorse him, it would have a dramatic impact on the election. The problem was how to get to Salb without others' noticing. Then Burt had an idea. He called Salb's office and made an appointment with his secretary to have his teeth cleaned. At the appointed hour, Burt marched into the dentist's office and told him to put away his instruments. He had come for something more important. The startled Salb said he wouldn't come out publicly for Burt, but indicated that he wouldn't kill himself working for the other side either.

Burt didn't even tell his running mates about the Salb affair, but some of his other activities did attract considerable attention. In late September he heard that the Republicans were having a street party in a garden apartment development. Burt decided to stop over and shake a few hands. Just as he got started, someone tapped him strongly on the back.

"This is a private party and you shouldn't be here," Eddie McDermott, the heavyset Republican boss glowered.

"This is a public street and I have every right to be here," Burt replied.

"If you don't leave, I'll call the police," McDermott shouted.

"Go right ahead," Burt urged. "You call the police and I'll call the press. Let's see who comes out ahead."

McDermott backed off, Burt continued shaking hands and people began talking about "the kid with the brass balls."

Burt was not always the one who initiated the excitement. In early October, he arrived late for a political coffee klatsch, one of dozens he had arranged throughout the campaign. George and Sarah Bach greeted him in their vestibule with expressions of alarm. The first problem was that only two people had shown up. The second was the two who had. One was a local hood with alleged mob ties; the other was his bodyguard.

The hood, a tall, wiry man with a sallow complexion, immediately cornered Burt in the kitchen.

"I can get you a lotta votes," he said, "but first I gotta ask you something. If you get elected and someone's planning to build a new restaurant, do I get to find out about it?"

Burt tried to answer as politely as possible. "When someone wants to build something," he said, "it becomes a matter of public record, and you or anyone else is entitled to know about it."

"That's terrific," the hood said and patted a puzzled Burt on the back. He asked a few more questions about access to information, got the same answer and left with a big smile on his face. In a small town where word travels fast, Burt heard within a few days that the hood had spread the word: "The kid who's running for mayor will work with me."

Burt wasted no time reacting. Using an intermediary, he got word back to the hood that he wanted no part of him or his help. It seemed the right thing to do, but it also made Burt a little edgy. "Somebody better start preparing my eulogy," he joked to friends.

Burt's message to the hood did in fact cause problems, but in a very different arena. A few weeks before the election he got a call from a local civic leader. The man said he wanted to come over and talk about some endorsements his organization was considering. Burt was pleased, but also a little worried. He had heard rumors that the civic leader and the hood were friends.

The night the civic leader came Burt made sure that his father was in the room, and he asked Vicki Lichtenstein, one of his straw hat girls, to sit in. If anything unusual was said, Burt wanted witnesses.

His concern was justified. The civic leader, a small, heavyset man in his fifties with a handlebar moustache and a penchant for chic denims, got right to the point.

"We like what you've been saying," he said, "and we're considering endorsing you. There is one thing, however. I've heard that there's a man in town who has tried to be helpful to you, and I understand that you haven't been very nice to him. I don't think it would do you any harm to—"

He got no further.

"I know who you're talking about," Dave Ross shouted. "That man is scum and my son will have nothing to do with him."

The civic leader's face turned red, he mumbled a few words and left.

Burt then turned to his father.

"Goddamn it," he yelled, "you better get one thing through your head. I'm the one who's running for mayor, not you. From now on, just let me do the talking."

With less than three weeks to go, the moratorium on high-rise apartments had caught on as an issue. Lawn signs and bumper stickers were all around town and Burt was increasingly visible. Still, the Republicans had not dropped the bomb that Max had warned about.

A small explosion did go off, but it wasn't the Republicans

who lit the fuse. Every Sunday night the Democratic candidates and a handful of others met at headquarters to plan strategy. As Burt saw it, the only purpose of these sessions was to create the illusion that the regular organization was calling the shots. The real campaign, he knew, was being conducted out of the Ross apartment. It was a delicate balancing act. On the second Sunday in October, it fell apart.

"I don't like the idea that your father sat in on our last meeting," Max complained to Burt. "He had no right to be there."

Burt's stomach muscles tightened. After a weekend of campaigning with a sore throat and tired leg, his limited patience was reaching its limit.

"Look, Max," he said, "my father has done more work than anybody, and he isn't a candidate. He's also raised money, which no one else around here seems to know how to do. You ought to be pleased that he's interested enough to come to a meeting."

Max could be as stubborn as Burt. "Don't tell me who's doing all the work," he shot back. "I work as much as anyone. And besides, that's not the point. Your father is not on the campaign committee and he has no damn business being at our meetings. That's that."

That wasn't that. "You know what you are?" Burt shouted. "You're a schmuck."

"Screw you," Max retorted.

Burt jumped from his chair and lunged at Max. The two wrestled briefly to the floor before others separated them. "Don't you ever say that to me again," Burt yelled while trying to free himself from the hands that held him back. "Then don't call me a schmuck," Max shouted. "Are the two of you out of your minds?" the peacemakers pleaded. "You're acting like children."

Tempers soon receded and the two grudgingly shook hands. Nothing changed. The campaign went on without incident. It remained firmly in Ross hands.

On October 17, the bomb finally dropped, but this time it landed right on the Republicans' heads. *The Record*, a daily countywide newspaper, ran the first of a three-part, front page exposé headlined "Fort Lee's Leaders and How They Got Very Rich." The series detailed how generations of local Republicans had "become happily wealthy while in public office." Myril Neiman wasn't involved in any of the land dealings *The Record* described, but his campaign was on the ropes. Corruption was now Burt's big issue.

When it came to organizing election day, Richard Daley had nothing on Burt Ross. Friends and fellow office workers came over from New York to stand in apartment lobbies and ring doorbells. Dave and Rose Ross and their friends were assigned to make calls from a bank of phones that had been installed in their apartment. Other people were working the phones in headquarters and private homes. Cars were standing by to ferry voters to the polls. Messengers were dispatched every hour to get the names of those who had already cast their ballots.

The rain poured during the morning rush hour and the big early turnout Burt had hoped for didn't materialize. "I don't believe this is happening," he kept saying as he shrugged helplessly and looked out the window.

Burt had as little control of his feelings as he did over the weather. He voted early then wandered aimlessly between headquarters and his parents' apartment. By noon the skies had cleared and he realized that he was getting in people's hair. He drove to Manhattan, checked in at the office for an hour or so, then went to a movie. He sat nibbling popcorn in the darkness, wondering what would happen to him if he lost. He had nothing to fall back on; he would be alone again.

Shortly after five he returned to Fort Lee with the rest of the commuters. He was just in time for a huge thunderstorm. He could see his people holding "Have You Voted?" signs at each highway exit leading to town, but the signs were drenched and barely visible.

It didn't matter. They came out and voted in the thunder and lightning and rain, streaming out of high-rise lobbies and making their way down treelined streets. Shortly before the polls closed at eight they were still standing in line to vote. It was an off-year election, and the turnout was an incredible seventy-five percent.

Burt stayed at his parents while two hundred people arrived at headquarters, standing shoulder to shoulder inside and spilling over onto the sidewalk. By eight-thirty all eyes were on the front door, waiting for the first returns.

Ellen Levine was the first to arrive. Her district was strictly tenant, and the smile on her face told the whole story. Neiman had gotten 167 votes. Burt had 415. Now the question was how badly the Democrats had been hurt in homeowner districts.

That answer came moments later when Mike pulled up with his score card. He was coming from a district which in previous years had given Republicans majorities of three to one and better. This year, Myril Neiman had 412 votes. Burt Ross had 483.

That was it. Two districts were in and by 8:40, the election was over. People began hugging and kissing. Horns began to honk. A few women reached for handkerchiefs. And old-timers like Pete McGuire, who had not known victory before, stood off to the side with dazed expressions on their faces.

When Burt arrived at nine, the happy shouting told him what had happened, but at first it didn't register. As hands slapped him on the back and people made way for him, he felt numb. He kept looking at the chalked figures going up on the tote board and asking, "How are we doing?"

Shortly after nine, someone shouted, "They're coming up the hill!"

The posh Republican headquarters lay at the foot of Main Street, a few hundred yards down from the Democratic storefront. Over the years, the Democrats had become conditioned to walking down the hill to congratulate the victors. Now it was different. Flanked by his running mates, Myril Neiman was walking up through the cool night. When he reached the door, the room grew quiet. Several people shook their heads in disbelief. They never thought they'd see the day. But as Neiman shook Burt's hand and quickly left, the final totals were beginning to sink in. They read Ross–6,344; Neiman–5,009. Mike and Max, not burdened by the residency issue, had done even better.

Now everyone was yelling for a speech. Burt got up on a chair. He said it was a great victory for the people and that the Republicans, who still controlled the council, had better watch out. Someone whispered that he should remember to thank the workers. Then also remembering that no arrangements had been made for a party, he invited everyone to his parents' penthouse.

More than five hundred people came. Democrats from neighboring towns, where the voting had gone Republican, arrived to drink with the winners. Fort Lee cops whom Burt had never met came to acknowledge their new boss. The New Yorkers who had worked during the day stayed until the last bus back.

At three in the morning, when the liquor cabinet had been emptied, Burt walked the last stragglers to the elevator and went to sleep. Fort Lee, New Jersey had a new mayor. Burt Lee Ross had a reason to get up in the morning.

5

On the plane ride back from a Caribbean vacation after his election, Burt met the woman he would marry. Laurie Miller was a twenty-three-year-old free spirit whose most serious pursuits were surfing, leather crafts and an occasional bit of amateur acting under the name "Brandy Williams." She wore T-shirts and jeans, had a bouncy sense of humor and didn't like politics.

Within a few months, Laurie had moved into the one-bedroom apartment Burt had taken in Fort Lee. She brought her movie posters, candles and health books in a suitcase that she assured him could be repacked on a moment's notice. She dressed Burt in mod clothes, put him on vitamins and insisted that he take her belief in reincarnation seriously. On weekends they went to Laurie's parents' home on Long Island, where her father baked pies, her mother danced to rock 'n roll and her younger brother made copper flutes for the Guru Maharaj Ji.

It seemed an odd match. Burt's relatives had suspected he would someday marry a tall, docile blonde who went to Smith and wanted no more from life than to raise a family. That wasn't Laurie. She was a five-foot brunette who had dropped out of Ball State, a college Burt hadn't even heard of. She could beat him in arm wrestling. She could outtalk him. And she didn't want children.

Perhaps like some others with overpowering personalities, Burt was actually relieved to be with someone he couldn't intimidate. "I can't explain it," is all he would say. "I only know that I've been with lots of other women and Laurie is the first one that doesn't make me feel trapped."

Laurie didn't like politics but she cared about Burt, and during his first months as mayor he needed all the support he could get. Max and Mike were outnumbered by Republicans four to two on the council, with Burt voting only to break a tie. There were no ties. The Republicans were going to let him know that they still ran the show. They voted unanimously against anything he was for. They smiled condescendingly at his frustration.

"You have to learn how to roll with the punches," chuckled Harvey Salb, who had decided to remain a Republican and was now out to prove his loyalty.

There were two major pieces of legislation—a high-rise moratorium and rent stabilization bill—that Burt wanted to enact during his first year. In the past the Republicans had conducted the biweekly council meetings before audiences of five or ten people. Burt soon realized that unless big crowds began to apply pressure, he was going to be a political eunuch. Laurie shaking her fist from the third row of the old, overheated courtroom in Borough Hall wasn't enough.

Before he introduced the rent law, Burt spent days on the phone urging people to attend the meeting. Nearly a thousand responded, and the council had to move to larger quarters in the high school auditorium. The Republicans weren't used to this attention. They squirmed in the spotlight. They said they wanted to help tenants but needed time to study the legislation. When they introduced motions to table, Burt wouldn't permit it.

41

"They're selling you out," he shouted to the audience.
The audience booed loudly.

"Vote now!" Burt yelled like a cheerleader.

"Vote! Vote. Vote!" the audience chorused.

One by one the Republican opposition collapsed and the rent bill passed. Little by little Burt gained confidence and took charge. The moratorium on high-rise apartment construction went through; taxes were stabilized; the police, fire and ambulance departments were expanded. A full-time borough administrator was hired. A master plan controlling the town's future growth was adopted. New recreational facilities were built. Senior citizens' housing was planned. A conflict-of-interest law for public officials was enacted. The entire government was reformed.

A year after his election two more Democrats got on the council, and they received even more votes in Fort Lee than Richard Nixon had. Now that Burt was in the driver's seat, he wasn't about to forgive and forget.

When Salb was booed during one meeting, Burt turned to him and said: "Well, Harvey, you better learn to roll with the punches." To another opponent he had just defeated, Burt smiled and said, "You have just been put out to pasture. Moo-o-o."

As he grew steadily more sure of himself, Burt began doing more of what came naturally. He had a small reservoir of patience and a large supply of comic put-downs. When he mixed them together, he came off as a political Don Rickles.

"I'm leaving now," Burt announced one night after he had grown weary with a meeting that had droned on past midnight.

"You can't just get up and leave," Len Kramer shouted at him from the audience. "You're the mayor of this town. You have to stay."

"Oh yeah?" Burt replied, getting to his feet. "Well watch this. Now you see me. Now you don't." And he disappeared behind a curtain.

Fort Lee council meetings were becoming the best show in town. People started coming who had no interest in government. Burt intuitively understood that politics was a form of theater, and he rarely failed to perform up to expectations. When he got bored during a meeting, he would reach under his desk and pull out a cowboy hat or nonchalantly light up a two-foot cigar he had purchased in a novelty shop. On other occasions he would look to the audience to provide entertainment.

"Aren't you an opera singer?" Burt once asked a man who had risen to inquire about a traffic light.

"Yes," the man said. "As a matter of fact, I drove directly here from the Met."

"Well, how would you like to sing a few arias for us?" Burt asked.

It could have turned into an embarrassing moment, but Burt had read the man right. For the next twenty minutes the thirty or so spectators who remained in the stuffy room on the first floor of a darkened Borough Hall sat in shocked silence as the little Greek tenor boomed out Puccini and Verdi.

Burt didn't use theatrical effects only to relieve himself; he also employed them to relieve tension. During the hearings on the high-rise moratorium, developers bussed in two hundred construction workers to protest that the legislation would leave them without jobs. Tempers were running high between those for and against the moratorium. One fistfight had already broken out in the audience, and the police had been summoned to maintain order. It was in the middle of all this that Burt decided to make an important announcement.

"I think I should inform you," he told the audience, "that a heavy snowfall has started outside and large accumulations are expected."

"Why did you say that?" someone from the audience shouted. "I just came in and it's not snowing at all."

43

"I don't know," Burt grinned. "The words just came to my mouth. I think it was because of something I once saw in a Danny Kaye movie."

The line produced a few chuckles, but Burt wasn't really after laughs. He had altered the mood and reduced the temperature in the room by a few degrees.

Burt's aggressive, offbeat style attracted a great number of followers, but by no means did they all come to admire him.

"Your son has become an albatross around my neck and I will devote the rest of my life to destroying him politically," Roy Sampath told Dave Ross one morning. Sampath's vow came after Burt at a Democratic Party Committee meeting called him a divisive hypocrite.

Eddie McDermott, the Republican boss, stayed on briefly as tax collector, but Burt attacked him regularly for having a no-show job. McDermott's political career ended in 1973 when the tax collector pleaded guilty to not having filed a tax return for sixteen years and was sentenced to six months in jail.

The police chief when Burt took over was Theodore Grieco, a stocky, hard-faced man who had been around for a long time. Years earlier, when "Tony Bender" Strollo, a hit man for Vito Genovese, disappeared, Grieco told the press, "He's lived here for sixteen years and has always been a good citizen and was never any trouble."

Burt knew that many of the cops on the force disliked Grieco but were afraid to speak up, so he decided to give them some help. He said the chief ran the department as his "own private gestapo," and that he permitted a "known underworld figure" to frequent his office.

Grieco sued Burt for libel, but several police officers found their courage and testified against him at a pretrial deposition. Grieco himself was then indicted for perjury, and the charges against him were dropped only after he agreed to an early retirement. Burt's reputation as a giant-killer continued to grow.

Landlords hated Burt because he had imposed limits on the rents they could charge. Developers sued the town because the high-rise moratorium prevented them from building. Republicans were up in arms against the kid who was driving them all from office. Democrats who had hoped he would share more of his power with them left the ranks. The civic leader had his private reasons for saying Burt wasn't doing enough for the town. And his friend, the hood, provided some unexpected comic opposition.

Crime figures ordinarily shun publicity, but the hood was a notable exception. Before going to jail, he frequently attended council meetings to register complaints. One night, he outdid himself.

"Mr. Mayor," he shouted into the microphone, "there's one thing I don't understand around here. You got the power. The developers got the land. And what do I got? Crabs?"

Many of Burt's enemies were stock characters out of Fort Lee's past. Others, however, were solely Burt's creations. In this latter category was a young attorney who was trying to carve out a political career for himself. One night during a council meeting the attorney objected to a proposed department store. It would, he said, "bring undesirable elements to our community."

"What's the matter," Burt asked him after the meeting, "don't you like blacks?"

"What are you talking about?" the attorney asked.

"Well, who the hell are those undesirable elements you referred to?" Burt asked sarcastically. "French?"

The attorney didn't answer, but Burt wouldn't let go. "You know what you are?" he asked loudly. "You're a racist, and I don't associate with racists."

No matter that while in college Burt had spent one Christmas Eve at Governor Wallace's mansion in Alabama. Friends of Burt who overheard the exchange complimented him on a command performance. But, at the same time, the mayor had gone out of his way to cultivate a new Ross hater.

For those who liked him, it was precisely that delicate area between honesty and abrasiveness which made Burt so attractive. He said things which other people wished they had or could.

Once a Swedish folk singer whom Burt had just met asked him if he had any contacts in the record business. Burt said he knew a couple of people, but he was reluctant to ask them for favors.

"Well, wouldn't you like to ask one for me?" the Swede persisted.

"No, I wouldn't," Burt said.

In a similar situation, most others would probably have said they'd see what they could do and then done nothing. All Burt did was tell the truth. Yet those who heard him talked about the incident for days.

By the beginning of his second year in office, Burt had shed the last vestiges of the "boy mayor" image, and by the start of his third year, the Democrats were in total control of Fort Lee. Max and Mike were joined on the council by four new members: Jerry August, a young insurance salesman who talked in comic dialects and told hecklers not to let their meat loaf; Jeff Kleiner, a school teacher who regularly pilfered Burt's desk for cigars and bet against him unsuccessfully on football games; Art Lauricella, a gentle-souled businessman who had worked on Burt's campaign; and Dick Nest, a barrel-chested accountant who supplied Burt with the kind of public support that a quarterback expects from a guard. Armand Pohan, a brilliant young lawyer whom Burt had known since junior high school, became borough attorney. Ted Hanser, the man who had first approached Burt about running for mayor, was appointed chairman of the planning board. When he resigned, Ellen Levine took his place. Burt's people were all around.

There was one exception. Pearl Moskowitz was a Democrat, but she had been nominated to the council against Burt's wishes. Burt respected the fact that, along with Max, she was the hardest working member of the council. But he had little use for a woman whose public positions, he was convinced, were motivated primarily by her desire to replace him as mayor. In a voice that seemed to straddle the line between anger and tears, Pearl opposed almost any kind of building. When she was told that those who conformed with the zoning ordinances could not be denied a building permit, she replied, "Let them sue us!" A year after her election Burt started attacking her publicly and the two stopped speaking.

Burt asked a great deal of the people around him, but never as much as he demanded of himself. He worked as hard on their campaigns as he had on his own, although he acknowledged that he was energized as much by an all-consuming need to defeat his enemies as by a desire to support his friends.

Nor was it all politics with Burt. He applied himself with equal diligence to the less publicized but more important business of running a government. His broker's job with L.F. Rothschild afforded him a great deal of flexibility, and Burt spent as little time there as possible. Fort Lee was where he wanted to be. He spent up to sixty hours a week working there.

On a typical day he would drive to Borough Hall at nine and spend an hour or so dictating letters to his secretary, Helen Cole, a widow who had known Burt's family since he was a baby. By three he would be back from New York in time to skim through the newspaper articles Helen had clipped for him before he performed one or more wedding ceremonies. Later in the day he would meet with department heads to warn them that if they kept going over their budgets he would start looking for replacements. After negotiating a sewer contract and being interviewed on cable television, he would drive home for dinner. At eight he'd be back at Borough Hall for a council caucus or planning board meeting, and when that was over, he'd find time to talk with a fire chief who wanted a new engine or a borough employee who had a drinking problem.

Of all his mayoral duties, the one Burt enjoyed most was performing marriages. He offered every couple a traditional ceremony or a more modern one in which he substituted East Indian love poetry for the Bible. The twenty-five-dollar fee he donated to charity. The power to say "I now pronounce you man and wife" turned him on. Even at these solemn moments he could not always resist clowning. Once when he spoke the words "Do you take this woman to be your lawfully wedded wife?" to a man about to marry a beautiful blonde, Burt answered his own question. "Because if you don't," he said, "I will."

Burt's own wedding, in June of 1973, took on the aura of an affair of state. "What's a nice Jewish Democratic mayor like Burt Ross doing with the daughter of a Republican Irish cop?" was the lead to the story in *The New York Times*.

Some of Burt's friends suggested to him that the eagerness with which he arranged four wedding receptions and his anticipation of all the presents which would result were not flattering.

"Oh, come on," was Burt's response. "I'm going to get married once in my life. I like parties. And I like presents. Now what the hell is wrong with that?"

Burt and Laurie were married on a deserted beach. Laurie wore a floppy white hat, held a bouquet of daisies and stood barefoot on the sand. In his sharkskin suit, striped shirt, butterfly bow tie and Panama hat, Burt looked right out of "The Godfather." Each of them wrote a poem for the occasion. Burt cried while the vows were exchanged.

The Godfather image was reflected in other areas of Burt's life. "Don't worry, I'll take care of you," was one of his favorite expressions. He enjoyed performing what seemed like feats of magic. When friends asked with amazement how he had managed to get them last-minute tickets to a Bob Dylan concert that had been sold out for months, Burt's only response was a cryptic smile and "Enjoy the show."

As much as he relished his image, Burt had the nagging sensation that the bottom line of his life made him a big fish in a small pond. Politically, there were no higher openings for him to chase in the near future. Economically, he was attracted to tycoons.

Nathan Serota was a multimillionaire and shopping-center developer in his early fifties who had been marginally active in Fort Lee's Democratic politics. He was a poor boy from Brooklyn who had dropped out of high school and worked for fourteen years as a railroad clerk. He started building houses on Long Island during the great suburban migration of the 1950s, and by the time Burt met him in 1971, he was reputed to be worth around $40 million.

Serota's lifestyle was that of a flamboyant nouveau riche. He and his second wife were preparing to move into a huge penthouse condominium with every conceivable convenience. He wore an expensive grey toupée. She kept her jewelry in a bank vault. They had a sunken bathtub. They got around town in a chauffeur-driven Rolls Royce.

In 1972, Nat and Vivian Serota began extending invitations to Burt and Laurie, first to their apartment, and then to expensive nightclubs in Manhattan, where headwaiters bowed deferentially as the couples were ushered to front-row tables. The specifics themselves didn't interest Burt, who got bored early and excused himself to go sleep in the back seat of the Rolls. The abstract power of money was another story.

Burt returned the Serotas' hospitality by urging Serota to get more involved politically, appointing him to the local Parking Authority and referring him to some commercial property in a nearby town.

The love affair didn't last long. Serota was accustomed to getting things his own way. With a strong-willed person like Burt, something had to give. When Serota started coming to council meetings, shaking his fist and screaming in support of the Mayor, Burt found it embarrassing and gaveled him into silence. It didn't take long for Serota's temper to begin directing itself at Burt, who realized he had made a mistake ever getting involved with him politically.

In early 1974 Serota reported to Miami Beach police that he had lost a grocery bag containing $60,000 in jewelry and cash that he carried around for tips and shopping. Burt started calling him "moneybags." Serota started calling Burt much worse.

Befriending Serota was not Burt's only error in judgment. Another was the frequency with which he met with developers who had business before the town. Concerned friends told him he had no business meeting privately with developers because it might be interpreted in the wrong way. Burt disregarded the advice.

"I meet with anyone who wants to meet with me," he said. "I know that the developers want to feel me out on my thinking and get on my good side. But what really happens is that I find out what's on their minds and that helps me anticipate their moves. It's a little like a chess game."

Why, someone asked Burt, would developers want to meet with a mayor who had won an election by opposing them and who ran a government which so consistently acted against their interests that fifteen of them were suing the town?

"Because I'm the only game in town," Burt replied. "They would do anything they could to get me out. But if they can't do that, they want to be near whatever power there is."

It wasn't as simple as that. The developers represented power far greater than Burt's, and the mayor enjoyed being close to men who commanded hundreds of millions of dollars, even if he could prevent them from investing it in Fort Lee.

Arthur Sutton was the biggest developer Burt met with from time to time. Besides his age and occupation, Sutton shared a great deal with Serota. He, too, came from a poor New York family, and after graduating from Bronx Vocational High School and serving as a combat engineer in World War II, he changed his name from Spinelo to Sutton and set out to seek his fortune.

When he chose his new name, Sutton may or may not have been thinking about Sutton Place, which in Manhattan is synonymous with great wealth. What was certain was that he devoted all his energy to reaching financial heights. In 1970, when he retired as general superintendent in charge of all construction for Arlen Realty, he was a millionaire.

Like Serota, Sutton was in no way shy about displaying his newfound riches. He, too, drove a Rolls Royce. In the spring of 1974 he moved his wife and two young children into a $750,000 home he had built for himself about ten miles from Fort Lee. He kept a helicopter in his backyard. He installed an elevator in his two-story house.

Sutton's retirement from real estate had not lasted long. In 1971 he had begun assembling parcels of land in the middle of Fort Lee, just a few yards from the George Washington Bridge toll booths. By early 1974 he had seventeen acres in all, and rumor had it that the price tag was anywhere from $20- to $30-million dollars. When bulldozers started razing the local movie theater, it became clear that Arthur Sutton had something very big in mind.

What that was, Sutton told Burt over lunch one day, was a $250-million complex that would be known as the George Washington Plaza. There would be four office buildings with more square footage than twenty-eight football fields; three major department stores; a hundred and seventy-five small shops and fourteen restaurants, including one that would rotate every forty-five minutes; a seventeen-story, six-hundred room hotel; two film theaters; a small playhouse; tennis, squash and handball courts; an ice skating rink and outdoor swimming pool; and parking for six thousand cars. The complex would comprise more than three million square feet with a potential annual gross of a billion dollars.

Simply put, the George Washington Plaza would be the largest project of its kind in New Jersey. It would tower over the rest of Fort Lee's neighborhood stores like the Colossus of Rhodes.

Sutton had just one small problem: he couldn't do a thing with his property, at least not without getting a dozen variances from the board of adjustment. He needed the land rezoned. He needed streets closed so he could build over them. He needed so many things that were prohibited by the current zoning laws that without the variances, his investment was worthless.

Burt listened to Sutton's grandiose plans with openmouthed amazement. It wasn't that he opposed commercial development. In fact, he considered it a far better alternative than apartment buildings for getting much-needed tax ratables. It was the enormity of the plan that staggered Burt. And the fact that Sutton had invested so much money with no assurance that he could get his variances.

Personally Burt liked the developer. Laurie had even danced with him at a political dinner. But Burt told Sutton that there was no way the board of adjustment would give him what he wanted. The traffic problems would be horrendous, he said. The whole thing was much too big. It would be like putting a blimp in a backyard. The whole town would be up in arms.

Burt was right. In early 1974 Sutton's attorneys filed an application for the variances with the board of adjustment. By the time public hearings began in March, opposition was organized and angry.

What Burt hadn't anticipated was who would be the drum beater against the project. It was none other than Nathan Serota. He put together a group called Fort Lee Aroused Citizens. He hired attorneys and stenographers to attend the board of adjustment hearings. He took out newspaper ads asking why Sutton would have spent so much money for land if he didn't have a commitment that his property would be rezoned. The implication was clear: Burt Ross and Arthur Sutton were in bed together.

At first Burt assumed that Serota was operating out of pure hatred for him. Why else would he go to such trouble and expense to oppose a project Burt knew wasn't going to be approved in the first place?

The answer came in April. A few weeks after the Democrats had chosen Mike Mosolino, Art Lauricella and a tenant leader named Lew Weinkrantz to run for council, an opposition slate filed for the June 4 primary. The slate was organized and financed by Serota.

The scenario was becoming clear. All of Burt's enemies had banded together to oust him. Serota was the kingpin and Councilwoman Pearl Moskowitz was ardently backing his slate. If they won now, Burt could be beaten the following year when his term was up.

Even Roy Sampath was in on the act. After his falling out with Burt, Sampath had started a weekly paper called *The Independent.* Now it became Serota's outlet. Burt was dubbed "High-Rise Ross." Sampath characterized him as the unlucky possessor of a "demented and warped mind."

It was quite a package the Ross haters had put together, and the ribbon around it was the Sutton project. No matter that Burt and his council candidates were on record as opposing it or that the board of adjustment was heading irrevocably toward rejecting the variances Sutton sought. Serota and his people had grabbed the initiative as the anti-developer slate and they were running with it. They took from Burt not only the issue that had gotten him elected three years earlier, but also the aggressive campaign tactics he had patented. They did mailings and left flyers door-to-door every week. They co-opted expressions like "concrete jungle" and used them as their own slogans. In a climate of carefully cultivated hysteria, they presented themselves as flower children.

In previous elections Burt had worked as though his career depended on the outcome. This time he acted as though his life were at stake. Like a roped bull being forced to its knees, he struggled to free himself from the builder-boss image. When he saw that it wasn't working, he began instead to exercise all his power as boss to get his candidates the votes they needed. He urged the board of adjustment to speed up its hearings so the Sutton project would be rejected before the election. He raised the bulk of the $15,000 limit on campaign expenses. He appealed to ethnic groups. He supervised mailings and spent hours at the printer, seeing that the headline type was big enough and making last minute changes in copy.

It had come full circle. In three short years, Burt was being transformed from a giant-killer to a giant. By the middle of May, with the election just three weeks away, Burt knew it was going to be very close. He was on the verge of losing everything.

6

Saturday, May 18.

When Councilman Mike Mosolino called him, Burt had just
come home from delivering campaign literature. All his efforts
were beginning to seem like a waste of time. For every flyer
Burt's side distributed, Serota's slate put out one of their own.
This week's was titled "Haven't You Had Enough Rossism?" It
had begun to seem as though printed words were no longer
going to change anyone's vote. What Burt wanted to do now
was take a nap until Laurie came home from headquarters and
then go out for dinner and a movie.

Mike said he wanted to come over right away to discuss something important. There was a note of urgency in his voice, but
Burt didn't attach any significance to that. Secrecy was Mike's
natural milieu. He could make a Little League dinner sound
like a CIA affair.

Mike arrived in work clothes and said he could only stay a few
minutes. Art Lauricella was waiting downstairs. The two of
them were going to put up some signs.

"So get to the point," Burt said curtly.

Mike paused, then looked around as though he were having
second thoughts.

"Uh, something just happened that was . . . I mean it was pretty strange, Burt," he said. "A guy came to my house and said he could bust up the other slate if we can get the board of adjustment to delay the Sutton vote for a few weeks. He said we don't have to get the board to approve anything, just to put off the vote until after the election."

Burt looked at him quizzically.

"What do you mean, some guy came to your house?" he asked. "Who was he?"

"I don't know," Mike said. "He wouldn't tell me his name. He just called himself Joey D. The only thing I can tell you is that he's not from Fort Lee. I would have recognized him if he was."

"Then what did he tell you about busting up Serota's slate?" Burt asked.

"Nothing," Mike said. "He just said he could do it if we can get the vote delayed."

Burt was irritated with Mike for either not telling him everything he knew or for knowing so little.

"Look," he snapped, "if you don't know what he was talking about or even who he was, what the hell am I supposed to do?"

"Burt," Mike said pleadingly, "I don't think you understand what I'm telling you. This guy didn't want to talk to me. He wants to talk to you. The only reason he came to me first was to feel me out about you, to see if you'd be willing to meet with him."

It made sense. Mike was a construction worker, an old-timer and a political hard hat. Joey D. was probably afraid to approach the mayor directly, and had picked Mike as his intermediary.

"What did you tell him?" Burt asked.

"I said I didn't know, but that I'd speak to you," Mike said. "The reason I came over now is that he said he'd call me tonight for an answer."

As Mike talked, two questions took center stage in Burt's mind: Who was Joey D., and what damaging information did he have on Serota's slate?

"Tell me," he asked, "what kind of impression did you have of him? I mean, what did he look like? How did he talk?"

Mike said the man dressed conservatively and seemed well educated. His description seemed to conflict with Burt's fantasy of an Al Capone, but it was still enough for Burt to bite.

"Okay," he told Mike matter-of-factly, "why don't we leave it at this. You tell him to be here tomorrow at two. Don't say anything except that."

Mike nodded and headed for the door, but Burt stopped him.

"Have you told anyone else about this?" he asked.

"No," Mike said.

"Good," Burt instructed him. "Make sure you don't."

For his part, Burt told no one of his conversation with Mike, not even Laurie. In fact, he had scheduled the meeting with Joey D. for a time when he knew she would be on volunteer ambulance duty. He didn't want any arguments.

Sunday, May 19.

Ordinarily, visitors to Burt's apartment building were stopped by the doorman, who then phoned upstairs to see if they were expected. It was because of this, perhaps, that Burt jumped from his chair when, without warning, his doorbell rang exactly at two.

Burt quickly put on some jeans, buttoned up his sports shirt and walked to the door. He did a slight double take. The man standing on the other side was wearing a dark blue silk suit with white stripes. His short black hair was combed slickly back. He seemed to be in his late thirties. He was about Burt's height but must have weighed forty pounds more. Yet there was nothing fat about him. His neck was short and thick and he had the chest of a fullback. His arms bulged from his jacket. Over one eye was a small scar.

As he extended his hand, Burt noticed that the man's fingers were incredibly thick and his nails, including two that were squashed, had been newly manicured. There was a large ring on his pinky.

"Hi," he said, "I'm Joey D. Nice to meet ya."

"Jesus Christ," Burt thought as he led his guest to the living room, "this is Mike's idea of a conservatively dressed, well-educated man?"

Joey D. asked for a scotch. While Burt poured it, he walked quickly around the room. He asked if anyone else was home and peered into the bedroom. He turned up the volume of the TV set, which was tuned to a Rangers play-off game. Then he spotted the tape recorder Laurie used for her piano lessons.

"That's not on?" he asked.

"Of course not," Burt said. "Why should it be on?"

After checking for himself, he took a quick swig of his drink, then reached into his pocket and pulled out two cigars. He handed one of them to Burt, who wondered as he lit up whether his visitor was being hospitable or had known all along that the mayor smoked cigars.

Taking another drink, Joey said the apartment was attractively decorated. He admired the view of Manhattan's skyline. He asked Burt whether the Rangers could go all the way. Finally, Burt gave him his lead.

"Mike said you had something you wanted to talk to me about," he said.

Now Joey leaned forward on the couch. His words seemed carefully chosen.

"The reason I came here," he began, "is because I think it's important for people to be able to talk to each other. Don't you?"

"Yes, I do," Burt said.

Joey D. relaxed. "Look, Mayor," he said, "it's incredibly important that the vote next Wednesday is delayed. I'm not asking you to approve anything, just to delay it. I'm telling you, it's a matter of life and death. If the project is knocked down Wednesday, people are gonna go to jail. Lives are gonna be ruined. You don't want to see that happen, do you?"

"No," Burt said, "but I don't understand. Why are all those things going to happen?"

"Believe me," Joey said firmly, "you don't know how big this thing is, how many people are involved. If the project gets turned down now, everything goes under. That's how desperate this is. That's why I had to talk to you."

By now he had said enough to make Burt feel concern for himself. Still, the curiosity lingered.

"I'm a little confused, Joey," he said. "You come to me and ask me to delay the vote, but you don't tell me who you are or who you represent. And you tell me that if I don't do what you want, the sky is going to fall in. Now, why should I believe you? How am I supposed to know that you haven't been sent here by the other side to embarrass me in some way?"

For the first time, Joey smiled. "No," he said, "I haven't been sent by the other side. Didn't Mike tell you what I said about the election?"

"Yeah," Burt said, "but he didn't understand what you were talking about and neither do I."

"I'm asking you to trust me," Joey said. "The only reason I'm here is because I got something I can do for you and you got something you can do for me. I'm what you might call a troubleshooter. They called me in a few weeks ago and told me about—"

"Who is the 'they'?" Burt interrupted. "The only person I know who has anything to do with this project is Arthur Sutton, and Sutton knows me pretty well. So if he has anything to say, why doesn't he come to me directly?"

"Forget about the word 'they,'" Joey said. "That's just my way of talking. Let's just say there was a fear of talking to you. Maybe it was because of the way you went after the old police chief, I don't know. You gotta appreciate that this is a delicate matter, that a lot of fear is involved. But my attitude is that everything has been fucked up, that you don't go into a project like this without sitting down and talking to the man in charge."

"Everybody can talk," Burt said.

"That's just what I told them," Joey replied excitedly. "That's exactly what I said."

"But I still don't understand what you're talking about," Burt pushed on. "What does it mean when you say you can bust up the other slate?"

"I don't wanna go into details now," Joey said, "But believe me, as sure as I'm sitting here, it can be done."

"What can be done?"

"The Serota slate can be busted up."

"How?"

"Well," Joey said, looking down at the coffee table, "what if someone on their ticket quit a few days before the election. That would really screw them up, right?"

"I can't believe that would happen," Burt said. "And anyway, what if it did? That would still leave two candidates, and they could still both win. So I don't see what's accomplished. What you're saying just doesn't make any . . ."

"Wait a minute," Joey D. cut Burt off. "I think I heard something outside your door."

"I didn't hear anything," Burt said.

"I'm sure I did," he insisted. "Go check it out."

Joey disappeared into the kitchen. Burt went to open the door. No one was there. As the two men walked back to the living room, Burt tensed. Joey's jacket had opened slightly. Strapped to his shirt was a pistol.

The anxiety which gripped the mayor had nothing to do with the fear of being shot if he didn't cooperate. It was like the moment a small child who has happily wandered away from his mother experiences when he looks around and realizes he is lost. Seeing Joey's gun changed everything for Burt. The fantasies, the adventure, the intrigue all disappeared. It suddenly occurred to him that he was in this all by himself and that he needed help.

When Joey D. picked up the conversation again, he was off on a different track.

"I don't know how I can convince you how important it is that the vote is delayed," he said. "I can see that you've got a real nice place, here, Mayor, but if you've got any kind of money problems, maybe I can help you out."

"I've got lots of money," Burt said uneasily.

"Well, I just want you to know that if money is any problem, it's no problem," he said. "People ought to be able to help each other out is the way I look at it."

The talk about money added to Burt's growing alarm. He wanted Joey D. to leave. He wanted to talk to the U.S. Attorney. He wished that he had never agreed to this meeting.

"I really don't think there's anything more for us to talk about," he said. "The board of adjustment is going to meet in three days and it's going to turn down all the variances. I can't delay the vote, and I wouldn't if I could. Besides, I don't see how delaying the vote by a few weeks would make any difference. The project would still be voted down."

"It would make all the difference in the world," Joey said. "Don't you understand what's going on? That land cost a lot of money and there are payments due on it soon. The banks know my people are having trouble getting the variances and they're running scared. They want their money now, but the money isn't there. Now, if we can just get a little breathing room until we work out something that's satisfactory to you, some kind of project you can live with, then the banks will ease off and the money will start to flow. That's why the delay is so damned important."

It was now clear that the delay requested was only the first step. Approval of the project came next. And after hearing Joey D. say it, Burt felt a little stupid at not having understood this from the beginning.

"I appreciate your problem," Burt said, "but there is nothing I can do."

"Anything can be done when someone wants to do it, Mayor," Joey said. "I don't expect you to decide anything now. I just need some kind of a sign to take back to my people. I can't go back empty-handed."

Burt had no desire to antagonize this man, but he wanted him out. So after thinking for a few moments he said, "Why don't you tell your people that I have no objection to meeting with their attorney after the vote and going over the legalities of resubmitting their application. Okay?"

This wasn't exactly the sign Joey had been looking for, but he seemed to understand that it was all he was going to get. And he seemed anxious to leave the door open.

"Fine," he said, getting to his feet. "I'll tell them that. But I want you to think about what I told you. Just remember what I said about money problems, because we can work out anything you want. Sleep on it, will you? I'll give you a ring tomorrow."

Joey D. walked to the phone and began writing down the number on the receiver, but that didn't fit in with Burt's plans. He was sure that the police would be at his office in the morning.

"Don't call me at home," he said. "I'll give you my office phone. That way we'll have more privacy."

"Beautiful," Joey D. said. "I'll call you there tomorrow."

"But how will I know it's you when my secretary answers?" Burt asked.

"I'll say it's Joe DiGiacomo. That's the name I'll use."

As they walked to the door, Joey stopped briefly and looked back at the television set.

"Great game, hockey," were his last words. "You get a lot of action for your money."

7

Monday, May 20.

From the moment he woke up, Burt was feeling paranoid. Instead of stopping first at Borough Hall, he drove directly to Manhattan, parked his car, and looking frequently over his shoulder, walked the block to his office at Fifth Avenue and 57th Street. There he paused briefly, trying to decide whether to go upstairs and call the U.S. Attorney from his office or use the pay phone on the corner. He chose the latter, and after losing a dime to a broken machine and borrowing some change from a stranger, he finally got through to Newark. Not that it helped. Jonathan Goldstein, the U.S. Attorney for New Jersey, was on vacation. Bruce Goldstein, his executive assistant and no relation, was in conference. Burt said he'd call back.

He went up to his office, paced around for half an hour, then returned to the street and tried again. This time Bruce was free.

Burt's message to Bruce was to the point. "I think I've been approached by the Mafia," he said, "and I'd like to come over as soon as possible to talk to you."

Bruce's response was simply: "Come in this afternoon,"

Burt had been on a first-name basis with Bruce, Jonathan and several of their associates for more than two years. Soon after his election he had gone to their office, introduced himself and said that he'd like to cooperate in any way possible. Burt had told them that he was aware of Fort Lee's unsavory reputation and that he'd like to change it. He promised to pass on any leads he came across.

During the next two years Burt had been in touch with them perhaps half a dozen times, usually to feed them rumors he had heard about people he didn't trust. Nothing had resulted from any of his tips, but his information had always been received politely and he had been urged to keep in touch.

Burt had nothing but respect for the U.S. Attorney's Office. With a staff of sixty lawyers, the New Jersey office was the fourth largest in the country. The four or five staffers he had met were all in their early thirties, bright and tough. When Burt made an occasional attempt to find out if they planned to act on anything he had given them, they looked at him as if he had just exposed himself to a group of nuns. They were formal, correct and played by the rules. That they wouldn't give him much more than the time of day made Burt admire them all the more. If they wouldn't play politics with him, they wouldn't play against him.

In fact the only political moves they made were to send crooked politicians to jail. Going after what they called "crimes of high public office" was their specialty. It was a tradition that had started in 1969 when Frederick Lacey was appointed U.S. Attorney and took his work so seriously that his life was threatened and round-the-clock protection had to be provided. When Lacey was appointed federal judge, Herbert Stern replaced him and continued the crackdown. In early 1974 Stern, too, was elevated to the federal bench and Jonathan Goldstein took over.

Among them Lacey, Stern and Goldstein had convicted scores of politicians, including a congressman, a mayor of Newark, nine other mayors, leaders of the state Democratic and Republican parties, the boss of Hudson County politics, two

64

New Jersey secretaries of state, two state treasurers, a State Assembly speaker and two U.S. Senate candidates. Some cynics suggested that anyone could have succeeded in New Jersey's sea of corruption. Burt knew better. These guys were dedicated pros. Every one of them was there because he had requested the assignment. During the five months of the year they were in court they worked seven-day, hundred-hour weeks. The rest of the time they slacked off to twelve-hour days and took Sundays off. Burt, who frequently had to defend his own hectic schedule to Laurie, sometimes wondered about the women who had married these men.

If there was anything that made Burt uncomfortable about the fifth floor office in the new sixteen-story Federal Building that rose over a decaying Newark like a phoenix from its ashes, it was the all-pervasive air of secrecy. Secretaries spoke in whispers. People scurried back and forth, their faces set in grim expressions. Emergencies competed with each other for attention. It was a place, as Jonathan Goldstein described it, "where there is no room for joviality or laughter." Burt's occasional wisecracks had never gone over well among these serious young men who were "doing the public's business." So somber a mood did they create that Burt often had the feeling while there that he himself was guilty of some unspecified crime.

On this Monday in May Burt arrived at around two and waited for twenty minutes before Bruce Goldstein could see him. Bruce had graduated Phi Beta Kappa from Rutgers a year before Burt had gotten out of Harvard, and had then gone to Cornell Law School. What made Bruce different from the other prosecutors was his cherubic face and a personality that Burt had found to be the friendliest there. It wasn't that Bruce told Burt more than anyone else did; it was that he smiled when he explained why he couldn't.

When Burt was called into Bruce's office, he was surprised to see that they were not alone. Bruce explained that he wanted Dick Shapiro, chief of special prosecutions, to sit in. This made

Burt slightly edgy. He had met Shapiro once before, and in the context of nice cop versus tough cop, Dick was definitely the latter. He was a six-foot-four former hockey player with curly red hair and a growing bald spot. He carried perhaps twenty extra pounds, but his style was lean and underplayed. He was the most tight-lipped of the prosecutors and conveyed the impression of violence under tentative control.

For perhaps twenty minutes Burt spoke uninterrupted. He told Bruce and Dick what had happened the day before, filling in the most minute details and repeating several times his conviction that Joey D. was in some way involved with organized crime. As a grand finale, he suggested that his phone be tapped, and he offered to wear hidden recording equipment if another meeting took place.

Throughout Burt's monologue Bruce and Dick had sat expressionless, looking directly at him in a way the mayor took to be total entrancement. When he had finished, there was a long pause. It was Bruce who finally spoke.

"Burt," he asked, "why did you agree to meet with him?"

It was phrased as a question, but it sounded more like an accusation. Its effect on Burt was to render him momentarily inarticulate.

"What do you mean, why did I meet with him?" he stammered.

"What I mean is simply this," Bruce said. "Why did you agree to meet with a man whose name you didn't know and whose motives you suspected? And why didn't you kick him out of your apartment when he began talking the way he did?"

Burt's stomach began to churn. He had come to Newark to be embraced for his courage and ingenuity, and here he was being asked to justify his motives. Even worse, he was finding it difficult to come up with the justification.

"Look," he finally said after a few false starts, "if I refused to meet with the guy, how would you ever know who he was and how would you ever find out who he's fronting for? I mean, if

I had said no, he would have just disappeared into the wood-
work, and maybe he'd surface again with some other public
official and you wouldn't know about it and neither would I. So
if you're interested in getting to the bottom of corruption, how
does it help if you run away at the first sign?"

Burt's response could not have been better. It threw the
challenge back in Bruce's lap. It didn't matter that Burt's answer had almost nothing to do with why he had met with Joey.
By now, having been attacked, he had started to believe it
himself.

While Dick continued to look at Burt through skeptical eyes,
Bruce answered, although he was not exactly responsive.

"Don't you think you're jumping the gun a little, Burt?" he
asked. "After all, what the man was primarily talking to you
about was some kind of political deal, and he wasn't very specific at that. It doesn't sound to me like he really offered you any
money."

"No," Burt said, "he didn't precisely offer me money, but as
I told you before, he brought the subject up several times and
kept saying that money was no problem or that we could work
something out. I'm telling you, there was no question as to what
he was getting at."

As Bruce and Dick sat there and listened to the mayor, they
were not unmindful that in the upcoming Fort Lee election
Burt Ross had a great deal to lose. And since most of Burt's talk
had focused on political intrigue, their wariness was under-
standable. After all, they didn't know him very well, and it was
not unheard of for a politician to manufacture an event, suck in
law-enforcement officials and then use them to his own advantage. Could that be happening now? Could this man who was
so quick to conclude that organized crime was involved, who
was so eagerly volunteering his services, be drawing them into
his own intrigue? Was it possible that his whole story had been
made up, that what he really had in mind was a press conference two days before the election in which he told the world

how he was working with the U.S. Attorney's Office to break open a big case? It was the kind of trap they had every right to fear, because if Burt was on the level, it would be a first. Never before had they handled a case or even heard of one in which a public official had stepped forward and offered himself as a guinea pig.

In truth, of course, Burt had no such political machinations in mind. If his motives were not as righteous as he had begun to believe, they were not as questionable as Bruce and Dick may have feared. What he was thinking about was Joey D., who for him was real enough. If he seemed a little too anxious to cooperate, it was an expression of his sense of adventure, not a need to con anyone.

"Why don't you do this," Dick suggested cautiously after Burt was through. "Why don't you keep in touch with us. If he contacts you again, let us know immediately. And if he calls you at your office, tell your secretary to keep a record of it."

On that vague and unpromising note, the meeting ended. Burt left with the sinking sensation that he had made a terrible mistake in meeting with Joey D. He had walked into Bruce's office as the champion of honesty; he walked out with his own integrity in question. He had come expecting to be greeted with reinforcements; he left feeling he was out on a limb and all alone.

As he took the elevator down to the lobby, Burt began to question his own mind. Bruce and Dick had seemed so unbelieving. Was it possible that his imagination had run away with him? Could he have completely misinterpreted what had taken place in his apartment the day before?

His sense of sanity was soon restored. Burt stopped in the lobby of the Federal Building to call his New York office. Millie, his secretary, said there had been only one call. It was from a Mr. DiGiacomo.

Tuesday, May 21.

The phone woke Burt at seven-thirty. It was Joey D.

"Listen," Joey said, "I'm sorry to call so early, but I tried to get you yesterday. Things are really getting desperate. I need something to tell my people. You've got to give me something."

Burt was tired and upset. After yesterday's meeting with Bruce and Dick he had lost all confidence in himself and what he had done.

"Jesus," he told Joey, "will you please leave me alone? I have nothing more to say to you. And you woke me up."

"I'm really sorry about that," Joey said, "but it's really rough on my end. Can't you do something to delay tomorrow's meeting?"

"Look," Burt said, "I told you before that I can't do anything. Now lay off, will you? I was up late last night and I want to go back to sleep. Good-bye."

Laurie, who was still half asleep, rolled over in bed as Burt put down the receiver and yawned, "Who the hell was that?"

Burt, who wanted even less now than before to tell his wife what had happened, said it was some idiot who was working on the campaign. Later that morning he called Bruce to tell him that Joey had tried to talk to him again.

"Okay," was all Bruce said. "Keep in touch if anything else happens."

8

Wednesday, May 22.

As on the day before, Joe DiGiacomo called at seven-thirty, woke Burt up and said the board of adjustment vote, now less than thirteen hours away, had to be delayed. This time, however, he didn't apologize for calling so early.

"Will you stop this," Burt told him. "There's absolutely nothing I can do."

"I've got to talk to you," DiGiacomo said. "You told me Sunday that people can talk to each other, and there's something important I have to tell you."

Laurie was beginning to open her eyes, and because he still wasn't ready to let her in on his errant heroics, Burt cut the conversation short.

"Call me later this morning at my New York office," he said. "You can tell me what's so important then."

Burt got held up in traffic on the way to Manhattan. When he arrived at L.F. Rothschild at ten, a Mr. DiGiacomo had already called. Burt dialed Bruce's number, but was told by his secretary that Mr. Goldstein was in conference.

"I don't give a damn where he is," Burt shouted. "Get him on the phone. This is an emergency."

When Bruce got on, Burt said that Joey was all over him. "I hope you remember," he said, "that the board of adjustment votes tonight. Now's the time he's got to make his move."

Bruce's answer was unexpected. "I've referred the matter to the FBI," he said, "and they should be in touch with you very soon. In the meantime, continue to keep me informed."

Burt was elated. This was the first sign that he was being taken seriously. The FBI! At last there would be action.

DiGiacomo called back at eleven. He didn't want to talk on the phone, he said. Could Burt meet him for lunch? Burt suggested that they meet at Rothschild instead, preferably around two. DiGiacomo insisted that he wanted privacy and it had to be at one.

Burt yielded. He didn't want to make Joey suspicious, not when he thought the feds were moving in for the kill. And he figured the FBI could handle a restaurant. DiGiacomo picked a place around the corner.

As soon as he got off the phone Burt called Bruce again to report on the arrangements. The assistant U.S. Attorney repeated that the FBI should be in contact any minute, but told Burt to get back to him if he hadn't heard from them by noon.

Twenty minutes later DiGiacomo called again. "I've changed my mind," he said. "Let's meet at your office. You must have a conference room or something. I'll be there at noon."

"Wait a minute—" Burt began, but DiGiacomo cut him off.

"Don't worry about it," he said before hanging up, "I'm already on my way."

"Jesus Christ," Burt groaned when he got Bruce out of another meeting. "He's changed everything. He's coming to my office and he'll be here in half an hour. Now what the hell am I supposed to do?"

Bruce seemed annoyed. "I thought you told me the meeting was set for one," he said.

"It was," Burt said, "but he changed it and didn't give me a chance to say anything."

There was a pause on the other end.

"Well?" Burt asked.

"As a lawyer and as a prosecutor," Bruce said, "I would strongly urge you not to meet with him."

"Not meet with him?" Burt said. "The guy is on the way over here now and you're telling me not to meet with him? That's terrific. Would you mind also telling me how to get out of it?"

Bruce answered in a slow, measured voice. "I am giving you the best advice I can," he said. "The FBI will be in touch with you soon, but until they are, I urge you to avoid the meeting. I don't know how I can put it any more clearly."

Burt was nervous when he hung up, but he was also angry. Where the hell was the FBI? Why wasn't anyone else as obsessed with this as he was?

He glanced at the wall clock. It was ten to twelve. He buried his head in his hands for a few seconds and thought. Then he walked from the large room where twenty brokers and their secretaries sat watching stock quotes glide across an electric sign.

Outside was a small anteroom in which the switchboard operator doubled as receptionist.

"Kay," Burt told her, "I'm going to be in the conference room. If someone named DiGiacomo shows up for me, tell him I had to leave for Fort Lee. Say it was an emergency. Also, try to get a good description of him and see if you can get his fingerprints if he touches anything. Call me as soon as he leaves or if the FBI phones. And try to act natural."

The switchboard operator either sensed the urgency in Burt's instructions or she was accustomed to brokers going off the deep end when the market was down. In either event, she nodded casually to Burt and asked no questions.

For the next forty-five minutes Burt paced the conference room. He chain smoked cigars and grew increasingly agitated. By twelve-thirty, he was feeling so frightened that he stepped out on an adjacent balcony. It was an odd hiding place: Directly below him, thousands of people mingled during their lunch break.

The phone rang at one. When Burt got to the anteroom, Kay said that DiGiacomo had just left. He had seemed very upset, she said. He kept mumbling that he had been held up in traffic. He had asked several times whether Burt would be back. And by the way, Kay said, reaching into a drawer and pulling out something covered with a napkin, he had made a call and touched her earphone. Here it was.

Burt had just gotten back to his desk when the phone rang. The man on the other end introduced himself as Denis O'Sullivan, special agent, Federal Bureau of Investigation, Hackensack, New Jersey.

Burt was so happy to hear from him that he didn't even bother to ask what had taken so long. He filled O'Sullivan in on the latest development, concluding with obvious satisfaction that he had gotten DiGiacomo's fingerprints.

"Do you want me to bring over the earphone?" Burt asked.

There was a chuckle at the other end.

"I don't think that will be necessary," O'Sullivan said. "When the time comes, Mayor Ross, we won't have any trouble finding out who he is."

Burt was disappointed that his efforts at playing detective were not appreciated, but he went on anyway.

"Then why don't I drive right over to your office now and go over everything in detail with you," he said.

O'Sullivan said he would be tied up for the rest of the afternoon. He suggested that Burt come in at nine the following morning. Burt kept pushing for the afternoon, to no avail.

He was crushed. Didn't the FBI understand that the board would be voting the project down in seven hours and that DiGiacomo and the people he worked for were trying to delay that vote? Didn't they want to be with him every moment between now and then?

O'Sullivan said he understood all about the vote, that he had spoken at length with Bruce. Still, he insisted, there was no great emergency.

"If their interest in the project is so great," he said, "I think we can assume that they're not going to give up just because it's been rejected once. They'll be back to you."

The logic escaped Burt. Once again he felt alone and insecure. He wondered whether it was possible that people still didn't believe him, and he decided that if he didn't get some support soon, he was going to lock his door and take the phone off the hook.

By three he was too distracted to do any work and too nervous to be alone, so he left Rothschild for Borough Hall. On arriving he went directly to the police chief's basement office. He wanted to talk to someone he knew would pay attention.

Arthur Dalton was a man Burt could trust. For more than twenty years Dalton had been at odds with the former chief, which in itself was enough to recommend him to the mayor. Yet in his own right Dalton was all one could ask from a local police chief. What Burt told him in confidence remained that way. He had never attempted to introduce politics into the running of the department. The men on the force respected him, and the mayor and council appreciated his efforts to keep them away from places he knew were potential trouble spots. For his part, the fifty-five-year-old chief with the ruddy face and fighter's nose respected the young mayor who had given him his job and had never asked anything but that he perform it well. And he took an almost fatherly pride in this kid who, like himself, had never shied away from a battle.

For nearly an hour Burt told the chief what had been going on, not so much because he expected help as because he needed someone to hold his hand. Yet when he had finished he found it was Dalton who needed comforting.

"Jesus," the chief said, a note of hurt in his voice, "I wish you had told me about this first. I know the FBI people very well and I know all about organized crime trying to muscle in on

Fort Lee. I could have helped you from the beginning."

Burt took pains to reassure the chief that no slight had been intended. He said that he had gone to the U.S. Attorney first because it seemed to be more than a local matter. He assured him that he had always intended to fill him in at the right time.

Burt's vows of good faith finally registered and Dalton's face brightened. He reached for the phone, called O'Sullivan, told him he was in on the case and repeated several times that Burt was a "good man."

"Those FBI guys are great," Dalton told Burt when he got off the phone, "and believe me, Mayor, I know them very, very well. I'm sure they'll take good care of you. In the meantime, let me know if there's anything I can do."

It was shortly after five when Burt left the chief and walked upstairs. His own office was on the second floor, and although Borough Hall had closed for the day and the lights had been turned off, Burt wanted to make a few calls before going home to dinner.

He had just reached the first floor and was turning the stairs when he caught a glimpse of a figure moving toward him from the shadows. Burt stopped, turned and froze. It was DiGiacomo.

"Hi, Joey," he said effusively, extending his hand and acting as though there were no one he had more expected to see. "I'm sorry I missed you at my office, but an emergency came up and I had to run over here."

"I've got to talk to you right now," DiGiacomo said.

"Fine," Burt said. "Just wait down here a few minutes for me, will you? I've got a call waiting upstairs and one or two things I have to do, and then I'll come down and get you."

"Okay, but hurry up," DiGiacomo said. "We don't have much time."

Burt walked slowly up the stairs, then limped as fast as he could into his office, grabbed the phone and called the chief.

"He's here!" he shouted. "He was waiting for me in the lobby.

I told him I'd come down in a few minutes to get him."

There was silence on the other end.

"Look, here's what you do," Burt said. "Send someone up here right away with a tape recorder and make sure he isn't seen. Then stay in your office until you hear from me."

Perhaps five minutes passed before a plainclothesman carrying a machine that looked identical to the one Laurie used to tape her piano lessons walked quickly into Burt's office. He put the recorder on Burt's desk and plugged it in.

"How's this?" he asked.

"How's this?" Burt said, throwing his hands in the air in disbelief. "What the fuck is going on here? Is the whole world crazy or am I? There's a guy coming up here and you want to put the tape recorder on my desk? Why don't you just shoot me now and get it over with?"

The cop mumbled a few words of apology, then put the recorder in Burt's drawer and tried it out. It didn't work. The mike wasn't sensitive enough to pick up their voices.

"Is this the only equipment you have?" Burt asked.

"I'm sorry, Mayor," the cop said, "but all our good stuff is out now on a narco bust."

Burt told him to take the recorder with him and leave. He wasn't sure how long Joey would wait downstairs, and he sure as hell didn't want him walking in on a scene like this.

Burt waited until the cop had left, then headed for the door himself. But just as he walked out, his phone rang.

It was Tony Cutrupi, a close friend of Arthur Sutton whom Burt had met several times and who contributed regularly to the local Democrats.

"Arthur wants to see you right away," Cutrupi told Burt.

"If there's one time in the whole year I don't want to see him," Burt said, "it's now."

"It's extremely important," Cutrupi said. "He can be there in a few minutes."

"There's no way I'm going to meet with him," Burt said, "and

I can't stay on the phone arguing. I've got other things on my mind right now."

Burt hung up and walked out the door wondering why, if DiGiacomo really represented Sutton, the developer himself was now trying to meet with him.

As he got to the hall, DiGiacomo was coming up the stairs. "Sorry I took so long," Burt said. "Come on in."

DiGiacomo followed Burt into his office. Burt sat behind his desk. Joey paced back and forth.

The pitch was the same as it had been on Sunday. The vote had to be delayed or lives would be ruined and people would go to jail. It was a matter of life and death.

When DiGiacomo had finished, Burt put his hand to his chin and shook his head. This was no longer just frightening; it was ridiculous.

"You don't need Burt Ross," he said. "You want Jesus Christ. You better hope for an earthquake, because short of an act of God, this is going to be voted down tonight. The board is going to meet in less than three hours and you're asking me to delay it? Well, I can't, and I wouldn't if I could. I don't control the board of adjustment and—"

"You appointed them," DiGiacomo interrupted.

"Sure I appointed them," Burt said, "but you don't seem to understand. They're just five nice people who don't get paid and who have been holding hearings on this thing for months. And if you think I can call them up now and tell them to find some reason to delay the meeting, you're wrong. I couldn't tell them to do it, and they wouldn't listen to me if I did. I've been telling you that since Sunday."

DiGiacomo didn't seem to understand what Burt had been saying. Or at least he didn't want to accept it. The mayor had the power. If he was holding back, there had to be another reason. DiGiacomo was going to find the key.

"Tell me," he asked casually, "what's your favorite place in America?"

77

The sudden shift caught Burt off balance, and he answered without thinking, "I don't know. I suppose Martha's Vineyard."

Now DiGiacomo walked toward Burt. He leaned over his desk and fixed the Mayor with steel blue eyes.

"I'll give you two-hundred-thousand dollars," he whispered. "You can live very nicely on Martha's Vineyard for two-hundred-thousand."

Burt flushed slightly. "This is crazy," he stammered. "You're barking up the wrong tree. I've already got that much."

"I'll give you four-hundred-thousand," DiGiacomo said.

"Forget it," Burt said. "You could offer me a million dollars and it wouldn't make any difference. I can't delay that vote, and I wouldn't if I could."

It occurred to Burt that none of this might have happened if he hadn't left the door open with DiGiacomo in the first place. But before he could figure out a way to make himself clear, the phone rang.

It was Chief Dalton, calling to say that Cutrupi and some other guy had just walked into Borough Hall and were on the way up to Burt's office.

"I'm really getting pissed," Burt said to DiGiacomo. "You tell me that you're speaking for the people behind the project. Then how the hell do you explain that Tony Cutrupi called me before and tried to get me to meet with Sutton, or that Cutrupi and someone else are on the way up here now?"

"I am speaking for Sutton," DiGiacomo said. "Those other guys are just panicking. Let's just do this my way. I know what I'm doing and those other fucks don't."

"Well, you go outside and tell them I don't want to meet with them," Burt shouted. "I don't want them in my office, do you understand?"

"Don't worry about it," DiGiacomo said, walking to the door. "I'll take care of everything."

As he disappeared, DiGiacomo left Burt with a number of questions racing through his mind, the most immediate of which was how to get out of this. But before he had a chance to think, the door opened. DiGiacomo came in alone and he was carrying a thick book.

"Cutrupi's here with someone named Orenstein who's very big with the banks," DiGiacomo said. "All they want to do is show you the figures in here so you'll understand how important the project is."

Burt would have liked to get a look at Orenstein, but he didn't want three men pressuring him and he didn't want three identical stories lined up against his. So as DiGiacomo started to leaf through the book, Burt cut him off. "Don't you understand me?" he shouted. "I don't want to see them and I'm not interested in whatever is in that book."

DiGiacomo started to say something, but Burt interrupted him. Too many things were going on at once for him to absorb. He was losing control of the situation.

"Look, Joey," he said, "why don't you go out for a drink with the other guys. Come back alone in an hour and I'll give you my answer."

A smile lit DiGiacomo's face.

"Terrific," he said. "I sure could use a drink. You just think about what I'm offering you."

When DiGiacomo left, Burt called the chief to his office. Dalton arrived with another cop whom he said could be trusted. The two listened intently while Burt sputtered out what had just happened.

"Isn't there any way you can wire me for sound?" Burt asked them.

"I'm sorry, Mayor, but our equipment is out," Dalton said.

First the U.S. Attorney, then the FBI, now the Fort Lee police. No one was coming up with the answers Burt wanted. He was still on his own, but he wasn't ready to give up yet. Not after the offer of a bribe. Not when he was on the verge of converting all the skeptics.

"Let's do this," Burt told the chief. "Call downstairs and tell

79

whoever is on the desk to make sure he calls me when DiGiacomo enters the building. Meanwhile, you two go downstairs and wait to hear from me."

Dalton made the call, then got up to leave. The other cop walked out ahead of him, but turned around and raced back inside.

"He's coming up the stairs!" he shouted.

"Shit," Burt said. "All we need now is for him to find the two of you in here. Is there some other way you can get out?"

"No," Dalton said.

"Then just leave and act natural," Burt said. "At least neither of you is wearing a uniform."

"I don't think we should leave," Dalton said. "Why don't we go next door to the conference room. Maybe we can hear what's going on."

Burt wasn't crazy about the idea, because if one of them coughed, the whole thing would be blown and it would be he, not Joey, who got caught. But since there was no time to argue, he motioned frantically for them to get moving.

The scene that followed immediately was right out of the Keystone Cops. Within seconds after Dalton and his sidekick had closed the door behind them, there was a knock on Burt's door and DiGiacomo walked in without waiting for an answer.

"I got rid of the other two guys," he said. "It's much better, like you told me, for the two of us to work this out alone."

"That's not what I told you," Burt said. "I told you that I didn't want them in my office and that I'd give you my answer when you came back. Well, my answer is still no. I can't do it and I won't do it."

DiGiacomo hadn't been prepared for this. "You've got to do it," he said.

"No, I don't," Burt said.

Again DiGiacomo started talking about the money. It would be the easiest half a million dollars anybody ever made, he said. All it would take was a couple of phone calls.

It was Burt's phone that rang.

He picked up the receiver and said hello. It was Dalton, speaking from the next room in a whisper.

"Get the hell out of there," he said. "Get out as soon as you can."

"Wonderful," Burt said. "Glad to hear it. Best news I've had all day. Yeah. Right. See you later. All the best."

Burt hung up and got to his feet. "Look," he said, "I've had it. It's past six and I'm going home. If you want to be mayor, you can sit in this chair and stay here. I'm leaving."

With that, he walked to the door, turned off the lights and left. As he went down the two flights to the police station, he heard footsteps behind him and a strange voice shouting something to DiGiacomo. The voice was saying, "Offer him a million." Burt never looked back.

Once downstairs, he slipped unseen into the police locker room and began walking the floor. There was nothing to do now but wait. He was happy that Dalton wanted him out before making the arrest. He wondered whether guns had been drawn and if DiGiacomo had been led away in handcuffs.

Twenty minutes passed, then half an hour. Nothing happened. When he could stand it no more, he opened the door, peeked his head outside and signaled to the desk sergeant.

"Oh, hi, Mayor," the sergeant said. "What are you doing here?"

"What am I doing here?" Burt repeated. "Didn't the chief come down with him yet?"

"The chief's in his office," the sergeant said, "but I don't think there's anyone in there with him. What's going on around here, anyway?"

"Jesus Christ," Burt yelled, "will you tell him to get the hell in here."

The sergeant left and returned a few minutes later with the chief. Dalton was puffing on his pipe. He seemed surprised to see Burt.

"I didn't know you were here," he said. "I thought you'd gone home. I was going to call you there in a few minutes."

Burt felt faint. This had to be the final skirmish in his losing battle with sanity.

"What the fuck is going on?" he screamed. "Didn't you arrest him?"

"No," Dalton said. He sounded like it hadn't even been a possibility.

"Why the hell not?" Burt demanded.

"We had no basis on which to arrest him," Dalton said calmly. "We could hear you pretty well, but not him."

"You didn't hear him offer me four-hundred-thousand dollars?" Burt asked.

"No," Dalton said.

"Then why in God's name did you want me out of there?" Burt asked. "I thought you were getting ready to bust him."

"That wasn't it at all, Mayor," Dalton said. "I just thought that since we couldn't hear him and you were alone in there, it would be smart for you to get out. There was nothing to be gained by your staying there any longer. And besides, you're meeting the FBI tomorrow."

Burt started punching a locker and shouting profanities. The chief puffed harder on his pipe and urged him to calm down. Other cops began congregating near the door to find out why their mayor was having a temper tantrum.

"But you don't understand," Burt said as his frustration turned to grief. "This was probably our last chance. The board of adjustment is going to vote in less than two hours. After that, there's no reason for him to come back to me. We just lost everything."

"I think you've got it all wrong," Dalton said. "I know all about his type. They don't give up that easily."

It took a while, but Burt's mood improved. Maybe Dalton was right, after all. He would be seeing the FBI in the morning. For today, at least, he was finished with DiGiacomo. But after the bribe offer, the shadowy presence of Joey D. could no longer be called a figment of his imagination.

Burt was still shaken enough when he got home for Laurie to pick up on it immediately. For the first time Burt told her what had been happening.

Laurie was upset, but not just because of the danger.

"The whole world knows about it but me," she said. "That's a really beautiful relationship we have."

Burt started to explain that he wanted to protect her, but he was too exhausted to put up a real defense. He left the dinner table, his food untouched, and was on the way to the shower when the phone rang.

"It's for you," Laurie said.

Burt wearily picked up in the bedroom. He was in no mood for campaign chatter.

"You've got to delay that meeting," DiGiacomo said.

Burt sat down on the bed. "You must be crazy," he said. "It's an hour before the meeting and you're still asking me to delay it? You need help, all right, but it should be from a psychiatrist."

"I'll give you half a million," DiGiacomo said.

"I don't want your money," Burt answered.

Now DiGiacomo's voice turned cold. "I think you better do it," he said. "We happen to know something about you that could be very embarrassing if it got out."

Burt's fatigue disappeared. "You know what?" he asked.

"Something that I'm sure you wouldn't want anyone to know about," DiGiacomo said.

"Are you trying to blackmail me?" Burt asked.

"I'm not trying to do anything," DiGiacomo said. "I'm trying to help you."

"You're full of shit," Burt shouted. "I don't know who you are, but don't you dare try to threaten me. If you know something, take it to the prosecutor's office. I haven't done anything illegal in my goddamned life. Now I've had it with you."

Burt slammed down the receiver, then picked it up again and

called Bennett Mazur, the chairman of the board of adjustment.

"Ben," he asked, "did a guy named Joey ever call you with regard to tonight's meeting?"

"As a matter of fact," Mazur said, "someone named Joe Green called me about a week ago. He said he wanted to meet me because he had some important reasons for delaying the vote."

"What did you tell him?" Burt asked.

"Well, he made it all sound so secretive and he wouldn't identify himself any further," Mazur said, "so I told him to get lost."

"And that was all?" Burt asked.

"Yes," Mazur said. "What's going on, Burt?"

"Look, Ben, I can't tell you any more right now," Burt said, "but I promise that in a short time you'll know everything. Just do one thing for me. Make sure everyone gets to that meeting tonight and that the thing is voted down."

"You don't have to worry about that," Mazur said. "It's been clear for weeks how everyone is going to vote. Ed, Dart, Dotty and I are against it, and Bernie's in favor. No one's going to change his mind now."

"Good," Burt said. "Just make sure nothing happens to cause a delay."

Laurie had heard enough from Burt's conversations with DiGiacomo and Mazur to get caught up in the drama.

"If Joe calls again," she suggested, "why don't you tape-record the conversation? It would probably be a good idea in case anything ever comes of this."

"He won't call again tonight," Burt said, "and when I see the FBI in the morning, they'll probably tap the phone."

"Well, just in case," Laurie said, and she started to wind her tape past the point at which she had recorded herself playing "Moonlight Sonata" earlier in the day.

The phone rang before she had a chance to finish.

Laurie ran to the bedroom, picked up the phone and heard a strange voice ask for Burt.

"Just a minute," she said, pushing the record button and holding the mike to the receiver. "Burt, did you get this call? Burt, pick it up."

Burt took the call in the living room.

"I am mad," he shouted after DiGiacomo had said hello. "If I ever get blackmailed by anybody, I'll go fucking to the U.S. Attorney's office."

The unintended humor in that line escaped Burt at the time, and DiGiacomo certainly had no cause to laugh.

"Burt, you took it up wrong," he said. "I tried to show you the consequences and details and importance of my conversation. You just took it up that way . . . I don't want no problems. You don't want no problems. You're making a big deal out of nothing. . . ."

"Look, my ears are pretty damn good," Burt said, "and I'm willing to listen, but I'm not willing to listen to threats of blackmail."

"Listen to me, Burt, you took it up wrong," DiGiacomo said. "I was trying to tell you that if the thing blows up, everybody gets hurt . . . I don't mean to hurt nobody."

"But I don't get hurt because I've done nothing wrong," Burt said.

"But I . . ." DiGiacomo started to say.

"And I am the mayor of this town," Burt went on, "and if the project is no good for the town, it's not gonna go through, and if the board of adjustment wants to vote down twelve variances, they're gonna vote down twelve variances."

"I say let them vote it down," DiGiacomo answered. "I'm not saying no. I agree with you, but all I'm asking you to do is extend it twenty-four hours. Say somebody got sick. Say anything you want, but it's critical to everybody that we . . ."

"For half a million bucks to delay it for twenty-four hours?" Burt asked.

"Please think about it," DiGiacomo said. "Don't make a rash

decision. You can make a phone call and help everybody . . . I'll come over and talk to you."

"No, I don't want you to come over," Burt said. "I'm not gonna talk to anyone tonight."

"Can't I talk to you?" DiGiacomo asked again.

"I am not gonna talk to you until . . . I will never talk to anyone who fucking tries to blackmail me," Burt said. "You either know something or you don't know something. If you know it, you better say it. Otherwise, stop horsing around."

"I'm not horsing around," DiGiacomo said. "Maybe somebody's bullshitting . . . I'll straighten the fucking guy out . . . I'm trying to be the fucking go-between here. I don't get another fucking dime out of this fucking thing . . . I'm trying to work with everybody to keep everybody happy. Let me ask you a question. You're saying to me, right off the top, okay, nothing was done with any of the projects that were in town?"

"That's right, never with one," Burt yelled. "We haven't issued a building permit in two years in this town. . . . Who paid me off? And what did they pay me off?"

"No, no," DiGiacomo said. "Nobody's saying that."

"You're fucking right nobody's saying that," Burt shouted. "You're goddamned right nobody's saying that. And if you know something, you better speak up, because blackmailing I don't like."

"I'm not doing that," DiGiacomo protested. "Will you stop it now. I'm trying to give you some information which was related to me and keep a few guys out of fucking jail, and in the meantime, I'm getting called a cocksucker. . . . My fucking name is on the fucking block here. I'm fucking wheeling and dealing and everybody's throwing stones at me."

"I think you better go back and get employed by somebody else," Burt said, "because somebody's gonna throw you down the river because they don't know what the hell they're talking about. Look, I'm not gonna talk with you tonight. I've had it. I want to take a bath and I want to think about life."

"All right," DiGiacomo said, "let me ask you one question, Burt. How are they gonna turn this thing down? Flat no, or are they gonna, can they . . . Burt listen to me one second, please. Maybe we can still sit down. . . . If you say that if they want to come in again or something . . ."

"Anybody has a right to reapply again," Burt said.

"But somebody's got to hear that in New York," DiGiacomo said. "I'm telling you, Burt, you don't understand this fucking thing. It's critical. You think I would be on you like this if it wasn't? I would see you tomorrow, the next day."

"Oh, these people must be imbeciles," Burt said. "Let them talk to a lawyer. Don't they have lawyers who can give them advice?"

"You're gonna be my lawyer after this," DiGiacomo said. "You're gonna be my attorney . . . Let me talk to you again. That's all I'm asking."

"Okay," Burt said, "but I'm telling you something. Don't you ever . . ."

"I apologize," DiGiacomo said, "and I'll straighten this cocksucker out that told me . . . Okay, so long. Calm down. Have a shower."

Burt hung up and walked to the bedroom to see whether Laurie had gotten anything on tape.

"Burt, first of all you didn't let the other guy speak," she said. "You just kept yelling at him. You didn't give him a chance to incrim—" She pressed the stop button.

Burt had no way of knowing it at the time, of course, but Laurie and her tape recorder had not been the only ones eavesdropping on the conversation. DiGiacomo had spoken to him from an office in a nearby town. Two men were listening in on extensions. One of these, in turn, had an open line to a much larger office in Manhattan, where two other men were anxiously receiving a running account.

What Burt did know as he undressed and waited for a call from Bennett Mazur was that the "whole fucking can of worms" DiGiacomo had referred to on Sunday was more like a keg of dynamite. For the first time it dawned on him that reality was running ahead of his own imagination. If the FBI didn't take over in the morning, he decided, he was going to treat Laurie to an unexpected vacation on some remote island in the Lesser Antilles.

Fifteen minutes after Burt and DiGiacomo ended their conversation, a more public drama came to its expected end. Mazur gaveled the board of adjustment meeting to order. After twenty hearings on Arthur Sutton's $250 million George Washington Plaza, the time had come to vote. Taking up the applications for the twelve variances one at a time, the board rejected each, four to one. The audience stood up and applauded.

9

Thursday, May 23.

For Burt, who had gone to progressive schools and whose parents had long espoused liberal causes, the Federal Bureau of Investigation ranked somewhere between Joe McCarthy and the Ku Klux Klan on his list of contributors to the quality of life in America. J. Edgar Hoover had not been a childhood hero.

The Hackensack office of the FBI was a ten-minute ride from Fort Lee. Burt's appointment was for nine, but he got there early and sat in his car smoking a cigar as the minutes slowly ticked by.

What he found when he entered the modern office building and took the elevator to the sixth floor was not at all what he expected. The room he entered overlooked a Bloomingdale's parking lot, a heavily traveled highway, a cemetery, and beyond, a wide expanse of treetops and sprawling suburbia. Inside, a dozen or so desks, most of them unmanned, sat in neat rows. Several of the desks had typewriters on them. Burt's initial impression was that the room could have passed as an insurance office.

If the office gave no hint of cloak-and-dagger activities, the two men who greeted Burt were even less evocative of the spirit of submachine guns and wide-brimmed hats. Special agent Denis O'Sullivan and senior resident agent Bernie Pirog were both in their early fifties. Both wore dark suits and conservative ties. Their gray, receding hairlines were combed neatly back. They had slight paunches. They might have been taken for Midwestern bankers.

But as they ushered Burt to Pirog's adjoining office, the mayor began to pick up some clues that he had come to the right place. He heard a voice talking in code coming through the speaker of a UHF communications system that was attached to one wall. He watched an agent who was preparing to leave turn a knob on an electronic device and then wait for an arrow to move to the green-colored area of the dial before opening the door. He saw the shoulder holster of another agent who had taken off his jacket and was leaning over a water cooler.

Pirog closed the door to his office, greeted Burt pleasantly and suggested that he tell them everything that had happened sparing no details. As Burt talked, O'Sullivan adjusted his glasses and took notes. Pirog interrupted occasionally to ask questions or wonder aloud about the real identity of Joe DiGiacomo and the people he was working for.

There was something about these two men that Burt found very reassuring. It may have been because they listened attentively and nodded their heads frequently. Perhaps it was that they seemed aware of Fort Lee's politics. In any event, Burt felt for the first time that he was being taken at face value and that he was on the good side. He concluded that all his preconceptions about the FBI had been wrong.

When Burt had finished, Pirog stroked his chin and leaned forward slightly in his chair.

"What I'd like to get from you, Mayor Ross," he said softly, "is your permission to tape any calls this DiGiacomo may make to you. The best way would be if he calls again at your home or office, try to get him to call back so we can be there to tape it.

Then, if he wants to meet with you, we'll make arrangements to be in the vicinity."

Burt couldn't sign the permission papers fast enough. What Pirog was asking him to do was exactly what he had been pushing for himself since Monday morning.

As Burt said good-bye to the two agents and drove back to Borough Hall, the only question in his mind was whether DiGiacomo would in fact call again. Maybe the board of adjustment vote had ended it. Burt didn't want that to happen, not after what he had been through. If DiGiacomo didn't contact him again, Burt feared that he would end up as the boy who had cried wolf. It seemed to him that he deserved better.

At Borough Hall he called his secretary at L.F. Rothschild, told her he wouldn't be in for the rest of the week and left instructions that if Mr. DiGiacomo called, he could reach Burt in Fort Lee.

With the bait out, Burt temporarily put aside one obsession and moved directly into another. He called Councilman Dick Nest's wife, Kay, a bundle of cheerful energy who put as much effort into campaigns as Burt did, and told her to make sure workers were lined up to distribute this week's leaflet. Then he picked up the phone and began calling people he had heard were planning to vote for Serota's slate.

"How can you do this to me?" was his basic pitch. "Don't you understand that Mosolino, Weinkrantz and Lauricella are on my side? If you vote for Serota's people, everything we've worked for is going to go down the drain."

Some responded to Burt's personal approach, but enough were noncommittal to feed his anxiety. The election was now twelve days away and still it seemed too close to call.

After holding a meeting to determine how much it would cost to put an end to the raw sewage Fort Lee was dumping into the Hudson River, Burt went home for a quick dinner with Laurie, then dashed out again to a cottage party.

Mixing with the thirty or so people who had assembled in an elegant apartment to meet the mayor and his candidates, Burt's fears about the election grew worse.

"Isn't it true that if your slate is elected the Sutton project will be approved?" a man asked him.

"Of course it's not true," Burt said. "Didn't you read the papers today? The board of adjustment turned the whole thing down last night."

"I read the paper," the man said, "but I'm worried that the vote was tied in with the election and that when it's over Sutton will come back and get it approved. I'm not naive, you know. It just doesn't make sense that Sutton would have spent all that money for land without a commitment that he could put up what he wanted."

The last line was right out of Serota's campaign literature. It brought acid to Burt's stomach.

"All I can tell you," was his anguished reply, "is that if Sutton got any commitment, it wasn't from me. I just wish there was some way I could prove it to you."

10

Friday, May 24.

DiGiacomo called Burt's New York office at nine and was told that the mayor would be at Borough Hall later in the morning.

When Burt got the message, he called Bernie Pirog, who came right over with O'Sullivan and a communications man. While the electronics expert attached a small suction cup to Burt's phone and ran a connecting wire to a tape recorder, Pirog gave the mayor some advice.

"If he calls and wants to meet with you," he said, "why don't you suggest Rudy's restaurant in Hackensack. That would be a very good place from our point of view."

Burt had never been to Rudy's, so O'Sullivan gave him directions to pass on to DiGiacomo. The mayor was worried that he'd mess them up. As time went by and the phone didn't ring, he was even more nervous that someone might still think he had made the whole thing up.

DiGiacomo called at eleven-twenty.

"Good morning," he began. "I'm running all over the goddamn place and I didn't want to miss you."

"My life's a little hectic, too," Burt said. "This goddamn election . . ."

"I understand, I understand," DiGiacomo said. "Is there any way that I can meet you, or can I tell you something over the phone?"

"Well, I'd rather meet than over the phone," Burt said. "Can you spring for lunch?"

"Yeah," DiGiacomo said. "You know where?"

"You know Hackensack at all?" Burt asked. "Maybe we'll go to Rudy's. Got a pencil and paper?"

Burt started to give DiGiacomo instructions, and when he got to one "on the right," O'Sullivan motioned frantically with his left hand. Burt corrected himself. "I'm sorry," he said. "It's on the left."

"I'll find it," DiGiacomo said. He suggested that they meet at one.

"Well done," Pirog said when Burt got off. "You're going to have to leave here in about an hour, and we'll want to get there even earlier, so we might as well set you up now."

Burt was wearing a mod brown corduroy suit. The communications man asked him to take off his jacket and shirt. He took a small stereo body recorder from his attaché case and, using adhesive, taped two tiny microphones and a small cassette to Burt's chest. Then he ran a thin wire from the mikes under Burt's belt and into a pants pocket. He explained that by keeping one hand in his pocket, Burt could turn the tape on or off by pressing a small switch.

Like the other men in his family, Burt's knowledge of electronics ended with the knob on a television set. So when he asked if he would be "transcribing" live, the communications man said no, that a forty-five-minute tape was being used and that the purpose of the switch was to conserve the tape for the most important parts of the conversation.

Burt wasn't very happy about this arrangement. "I'm going to have enough things on my mind," he said, "without having to worry about whether I've just turned the thing on or off."

"All right," Pirog said softly, as though it were a matter of no consequence. "Forget about it. Once you've turned it on, leave it alone. I'm sure we'll get everything we need."

As Burt stood there bare-chested, getting wired and surrounded by three men, the door to his office opened.

"What is it, Helen?" he asked his secretary, with a twinge of regret that he hadn't confided in her before.

"It can wait," said the woman whom Burt would have trusted with the secret to the H-Bomb. "Someone's here who wants to talk to you about bids for a sewer contract, but I'll tell him you're tied up." Without batting an eyelash, she turned and walked from the room.

"What a woman," Burt said when she had left.

"You don't think that will cause any problems?" Pirog asked.

"All your agents should be as closemouthed," Burt said.

With the taping device installed and tested, the conversation turned to the meeting itself. Pirog asked Burt to find out everything he could about DiGiacomo, the people he was working with and what they wanted.

"Try to get as specific information as possible," he urged, "and see if you can get a meeting with Sutton. Tell DiGiacomo you're tired of meeting with him, that he's a small-fry and if they expect you to deal, you want to see the man at the top."

"I know you haven't seen DiGiacomo yet," Burt said with a nervous laugh, "but I have, and believe me, I'm not about to call him a small-fry to his face."

"I'm sure you can do it tactfully," Pirog said, "and don't be worried. Denis and I and a few others will be at a table nearby, and we'll have plenty of other people in the area. Just try not to look at us. He may have someone there watching you."

The three agents left to set themselves up. Burt lingered at Borough Hall for another half hour, telling Helen not to be concerned, that he would explain everything to her as soon as he could.

On his way out he stopped outside Chief Dalton's office. He wanted to tell the chief that he'd speak to him later in the day, but he paused before entering. Someone inside was playing the piano.

The music sounded vaguely familiar. Burt walked in, took one look and burst into laughter. Dalton and a detective were hunched over the tape recording Laurie had made Wednesday night, puzzled expressions on their faces.

"There must be some mistake, Mayor," Dalton said. "I turned this on and—"

"Maybe you just don't like classical music," Burt said, "but the Moonlight Sonata is really exciting. Keep listening. It gets better and better."

It was a minute or two after one when Burt found his way to Rudy's and parked the '64 Chevy he had driven since college. Two men sitting in a gray station wagon seemed to be looking him over, but Burt wasn't sure which side they were on and pretended not to notice.

As he reached the white stucco front, a maroon Continental cruised up to him and DiGiacomo waved from it. Burt returned the greeting, then walked in without waiting for Joey to park. He was ushered immediately to a table in the rear. As his eyes adjusted to the subdued lighting, he noticed the table diagonally across from him, perhaps ten feet away. Pirog and O'Sullivan were sitting with two other men, all of them working their drinks and looking for all the world like they were having a business lunch. And so they were.

Burt glanced quickly at them, but they didn't look up. To avoid further temptation, he sat with his back to them. Were they close enough, he wondered, to hear him live?

A few minutes later DiGiacomo came in, looked around until he spotted Burt and walked over. He shook Burt's hand before sitting down, then ordered a double scotch. Burt, who had never been a drinker, asked for a Bloody Mary.

DiGiacomo said he liked Italian restaurants. Burt said the food here was pretty good. Then the drinks arrived, DiGiacomo took a swig and got right to it. Burt slowly slid his hand into the left side pocket and pushed the switch.

"I started to explain what our problem was the last time I spoke to you," DiGiacomo began, "and it wasn't the right atmosphere for doing it. I was under pressure and I know you didn't appreciate it, but believe me, I don't operate in that style and I don't think the other guy does, but we got a serious problem. When a guy is sinking, he'll grab onto anything he can get into . . ."

"Let me get one thing straight," Burt said, "because ya know, I have everything to lose. But let's be clear. I'm a public official, come from a good family. I got everything to lose and you come . . . you know, for all intents and purposes, I don't know who you are. Joe who?"

DiGiacomo smiled and came out of the closet.

"You don't know who I am?" he asked. "I can tell you who I am. Joe Diaco. D–I–A–C–O."

The name had no more meaning to Burt than the others had.

"Okay, Joe Diaco," he said, "but the point is that I can know Joe Diaco, Joe DiGiacomo, Joey D. That isn't the point. I never saw your face before. Now you say you represent him. Where are you from? How do . . ."

"In other words," Diaco interrupted, "if the project goes, I get a piece of the construction. I would say I'm a contractor. Okay?"

"Now, are you speaking for Sutton?" Burt asked.

"Yes," Diaco said.

"Does Sutton know you exist?" Burt persisted, "or am I talking to somebody out of the blue?"

"No, no," Diaco said. "We're talking Sutton. Sutton knows that I was going to call you today. He knows that I was gonna meet you."

Just then a waitress walked by and Burt must have looked up at her because Diaco nudged him in the side.

"You like that, huh?" he asked.

"I'm married, but I can look," Burt said. "Look but no touch."

"Because if you want to touch, that's easy," Diaco said. "I gotta couple of blondes in East Orange that would make your hair stand."

"My wife's uppercut can make my hair stand," Burt said. "Thank you, but no thank you."

His offer rejected, Diaco returned to convincing Burt that he really did represent Sutton.

"He knows," Diaco said. "I've helped him on some other things. The only thing that I'm sorry for is that he didn't tell me sooner. You see . . . he's got this thing so fouled up, in my opinion, and it wasn't guided properly and that's what he needs. He needs to be told what to do and how to do it and I really can't understand how things are so fucked up. I really mean it. You know, like you said to me the other day, how can a guy commit so much money and not have a thing?"

"That's right," Burt said. "How does he answer that?"

"He answers that by saying he had a commitment," Diaco said.

"But who the hell gave him the commitment?" Burt asked.

"The other administration," Diaco said.

"The other administration?" Burt repeated incredulously. "But we've been in power for two years . . . and I hear from you less than a week before the thing is finally voted on? It doesn't make sense."

"Well, because when I was brought into it, okay, the big problem was that they felt that you weren't going along with it, okay, or looking at it objectively," Diaco said.

"Joe, Joe, I'm sorry," Burt cut in. "When you say 'they,' now I just want to make sure whom I'm talking to. That's the point."

"I'm representing Sutton," Diaco said.

"Well, then, that's not a 'they,' that's a 'he,' " Burt said.

"Well, I say 'they,' I mean Sutton," Diaco insisted. "Let's say Art from now on, okay?"

"Okay," Burt said, "now why hasn't he spoken to me directly? Why does he send somebody who isn't on my level. I'm not saying you are on a lower level. He's a businessman. I'm a businessman. Why doesn't he come and talk to me?"

"How can I answer that question?" Diaco said. "You want an answer to the way I feel? It seems to me that every time there's a crucial decision . . . I'm not cutting the guy down, ya know, everybody's got their own makeup . . . every time there's an important thing, there's something that has to be done immediately, it seems they always put somebody in the front, not to make the decision, but to talk or to receive information. And that's the kind of makeup I got . . . Because personally, I think the guy's a nice guy, ya know what I mean, as an individual. He's trying to do the right thing, but he . . ."

"But he sends somebody who doesn't have to lose what I have to lose," Burt cut in.

"Mr. Mayor, listen to me," Diaco said. "Here's what you're not thinking about. You're not thinking about that he's got his fucking house to worry about, somebody else's house, the banker's house to lose."

Diaco wasn't making much sense.

"But the point is this," Burt said. "You can make me an offer . . . if something goes wrong, I lose, you lose and he, he don't know from nothing. He never saw you. He never saw me. And that's fine for him."

"I can clear that up," Diaco said. "Look, you want it that way, it's all right with me. I don't care. I'm trying to do whatever has to be done in order to make it right."

Now that it seemed that Sutton would come out in the open, Burt turned his attention to other items. Diaco appeared more willing to talk now, and Burt wanted to get as much on tape as possible.

"Last Wednesday," he said, ". . . I get a call just the same time you were in my office from Tony Cutrupi, who tells me, he says he wants to see me. . . . I say, ya know, not today. And then, five minutes later, he comes in with some guy whom I never heard of . . ."

"His name is Orenstein," Diaco volunteered. "He's with First Investors. Donald Orenstein."

"First Investors?" Burt asked.

"I said First Investors?" Diaco corrected himself. "I meant to say Investors Funding."

The name registered slightly with Burt. He knew that Investors Funding handled real estate and that it owned some property in Fort Lee. He had also heard rumors that the company had loaned Sutton money for his project, but that was about it. When Burt asked a few more questions, Diaco either didn't know the answers or didn't want to talk. Not wanting to push his luck, Burt dropped the subject and moved on. He was beginning to worry about how long the tape would last, and they still hadn't talked about money.

"Let me ask you something," he said. "You come to me last Wednesday. You offer five-hundred-thousand dollars to stop, to delay it. Now if I had delayed it a week or two, you could have come back a day later and said it's been nice knowing you . . . Those two women in the Oranges I appreciate, but that to me isn't good faith. Not when we're talking about a quarter-of-a-billion-dollar project."

Diaco looked around, then leaned toward Burt.

"A hundred thousand in green," he said softly. "Is that good faith?"

"That's different," Burt said. "That's good faith."

"But it don't get spent until it's done," Diaco said. "Understand?"

"I couldn't spend it if I wanted to," Burt said, "but I hold it."

"Okay," Diaco said. "Boy, whoever fixed that drink was loaded. If we don't get this done now . . . either by the planning board or through the board of adjustment . . . the rug is going to be pulled out. Investors Funding is going to go bankrupt. If the thing is done before June 17, all the money gets loose to the land and the money starts to flow."

"But you told me just a couple of days ago that that was all going to happen Wednesday," Burt said. "Now, it's not happened. It didn't happen Wednesday. Now it's gonna happen on June 17 ... How am I going to get something done by June 17?"

"Well, we're going to present a new plan, right, a modified plan," Diaco said. He started to describe the scaled-down version that Sutton wanted passed, but it soon became apparent that he didn't know the details. All he knew was that it still had to be big enough for Sutton to get a return on his investment. And that investment, he hinted obliquely, included money that had been spent to grease someone else's palm.

Burt's ears perked up. "Let me get something straight," he said. "If they've been dealing with people in my government without my knowing it, then I don't like it."

"Listen, what I do with you, nobody knows," Diaco said. "You got my word."

"That isn't the point," Burt said. "I don't want to be sharing with somebody . . . but you're telling me the money's already been spent."

"I can tell you without too much reservation," Diaco said, "it's not on your side."

"But there ain't nobody on the other side," Burt said.

"How about the objectors?" Diaco asked.

Burt shook his head. "That's tough to believe," he said. "I just find that . . ."

"Take my word for it," Diaco said. "I know what I'm talking about. These are things I hesitate to tell you."

"Serota's got so much money, the guy's got forty-three million dollars," Burt said. "I mean, it just doesn't, it just doesn't make sense."

Diaco wouldn't elaborate, and the little he had suggested seemed so patently insane that Burt began to worry whether anything this man had said was true.

"I may be better off meeting with Sutton," he said.

"If you want, I can set it up," Diaco said. "If you want me to be there, I'll be there . . . how about Sunday morning?"

Burt told Diaco to call him at Borough Hall around five to confirm. "I want to talk to Sutton," he said. "I want him to tell it to me intelligently . . ."

Once again Diaco asked how quickly Burt could get the project through the board of adjustment.

"I gotta do a little research," Burt answered. "Right now you're at me in my busiest season, you know, ten days before an election."

"I think they made a mistake pushing it before the election," Diaco said. "I don't think they had any choice . . . that's my only explanation. You know, I don't ask that many questions. I try and do what's right."

"Okay," Burt said, "but you know who you're working with, who you're working for. I didn't and that's the difference. You just come out of the blue telling one guy you're Joe Green, another guy you're Joe D. and another guy you're Joe DiGiacomo."

Diaco laughed. "You want one of my cards?"

"It doesn't matter," Burt said.

Diaco reached into his wallet, pulled out a small white business card and handed it to Burt. "Don't lose it," he said.

Without looking at it, Burt put the card in his jacket pocket and rose to leave.

"I gotta get home, back to work," he said. "I am so tired. Everybody calls me at weird hours . . . I tell ya, some of this doesn't make sense to me."

"Listen to what I say," Diaco said. "I ain't bullshitting you. I got nothing to gain by bullshitting you."

Burt and Diaco walked out of the restaurant together, past the table where Pirog, O'Sullivan and their two companions were just getting their coffee. Burt looked straight ahead.

Outside Diaco shook Burt's hand, said he'd call later and walked to his car. Burt drove around side streets before making his way to the FBI office two miles away. For the second time in two days he entertained the fantasy of Diaco's being arrested.

This time it was short-lived. He remembered after a few minutes that the conversation had not been transmitted live. And with all the noise in the restaurant he knew that Pirog and O'Sullivan could not have overheard it.

It was almost two-thirty when Burt parked, as Pirog had instructed him, on the second level of an open-tiered lot between the FBI office and a grassy knoll. While he waited anxiously for the others to return, he had to relieve himself and walked behind a clump of bushes near his car. Standing there, he reached absentmindedly into his jacket pocket and felt something. He pulled out the small white card and looked at it. On the top was a red heart. Printed below were the words

Valentine Electric Company
Belleville, New Jersey
Joseph Diaco, Vice President

The name Valentine Electric sounded vaguely familiar to Burt. As he put the card back in his pocket, he thought that he might have seen their sign on a construction site in Fort Lee. Then his mind wandered and he formed another association. It was with the Saint Valentine's Day Massacre.

Perhaps ten minutes passed before Pirog's car pulled up the ramp, stopped briefly, then pulled up next to Burt. The four agents inside got out of their car, walked directly to the mayor and formed a huddle around him.

When they took off his jacket and shirt and removed the tape and mikes, Burt's body relaxed.

"How'd I do?" he asked.

"It looked good from where we were," Pirog said, "but we couldn't hear anything. Let's get into our car and check it out."

The five men piled into Pirog's black Plymouth. O'Sullivan put the tape into a cassette player. Pirog put on a set of headphones. Then he pushed the "play" button.

What Burt heard sounded like a recording that had been made in a crowded locker room after a big victory. Voices overlapped each other. The clinking of glasses and other background noises made it almost impossible to hear the conversation. A constant crackling sound made it even worse. Burt's heart began to sink as he looked at Pirog's impassive face.

A few minutes passed before Pirog turned the tape off and removed his head set.

"Terrific," he said. "It sounds real good."

"I don't get it," Burt said. "I couldn't hear a thing."

"The other noises are no problem," Pirog assured him. "We have a filtering system and amplifiers to clean it up. Take my word for it, this is going to come out just fine."

Burt sighed with relief. He started to tell the agents what was on the tape, then remembered that Diaco was going to call him later in the afternoon.

"Diaco said he'd call me at Borough Hall around five to confirm a meeting with Sutton," Burt said, "and I think . . ."

"Diaco?" Pirog cut in.

"Oh, Christ," Burt said, "with everything going on I forgot to tell you. He gave me his real name. It's Joseph Diaco. Here. He gave me this."

Burt pulled the card out of his pocket and handed it to Pirog. The agent stared at it for a few moments, then passed it around. Suddenly all four agents were nodding to each other and smiling. In fact, they seemed ecstatic.

"What's going on?" Burt asked.

O'Sullivan patted Burt on the shoulder. The expression on his face had changed completely. It was now filled with admiration.

"He's for real," he said. "We've got ourselves a big one."

"You know who he is?" Burt asked.

"We certainly do," Pirog said happily. "We didn't recognize him at Rudy's, but we sure know who he is now."

And so they did. Joseph Diaco was the number-two man in a company that had been repeatedly cited as having ties with organized crime. Until his indictment in 1970 with then Newark Mayor Hugh Addonizio on extortion and conspiracy charges, Anthony "Tony Boy" Boiardo had been another partner in Valentine Electric. Boiardo and his father, Ruggiero "Richie the Boot," were reputed captains or "caporegimas" in northern New Jersey's biggest crime family, that of the late Vito Genovese.

The elder Boiardo was a prohibition racketeer who allegedly graduated to gang overlord of all the numbers action in New Jersey and part of New York. According to FBI transcripts of bugged conversations, another crime chieftain said "The Boot" had once bragged of killing Anthony "Tony Bender" Strollo, a hit man for Genovese who lived in Fort Lee until he left his home one day to buy a paper and never returned.

After a gambling and conspiracy trial in the early 1970s that resulted in additional convictions for jury tampering, "The Boot" served two and one-half years in prison. When he got out he retired to his palatial estate to contemplate the imported stone statues he had had made in the image of other family members.

"Tony Boy's" bust must have loomed the largest. By the 1960s the younger Boiardo had begun taking on more and more family duties. FBI tapes revealed that he had once threatened to break the legs of someone who complained about having to give kickbacks. When he was indicted with Addonizio, Valentine Electric announced that it had severed all ties with him. Federal authorities didn't seem too impressed. When it was learned that the U.S. Attorney's office in Newark had been wired for electricity by Valentine, the whole place was checked out for bugs.

Despite its reputation, or perhaps because of it, Valentine Electric continued to do millions of dollars' worth of work throughout the state. A new high-rise luxury building in Fort Lee had been just one of the company's lucrative contracts.

It was not surprising, then, that when Pirog and the other agents looked at the card Burt had given them, the name Valentine Electric did more than register. They knew all about Joseph Diaco and the company's president, Andy Valentine. And they were elated that Diaco was more than a small-fry.

So was Burt. His first reactions showed neither fear nor even concern, just delight that he had been right from the beginning, that he had been the first to say that Joey D. was someone special, that he would at last be taken seriously. As they rode the elevator together for a debriefing in Pirog's office, Burt sensed that the whole mood had changed. No longer was he being treated cordially. Now he was one of them, a full-fledged partner on a big-game expedition.

Pirog called Bruce Goldstein to report on the meeting, and although he talked with professional cool, he was clearly excited. Burt had the distinct impression that the executive assistant U.S. Attorney was similarly impressed. When he had finished with Bruce, Pirog turned to Burt and said he'd be at Borough Hall well before five. He joked that agents would resent having to work on Memorial Day weekend, but if that was the best time for Sutton, he was sure they would be happy to cancel their other arrangements.

Burt got back to Borough Hall around three-thirty. In the hour before the agents came to set up the taping equipment he tried unsuccessfully to distract himself with town business. The borough administrator tried to talk to him about new insurance rates for town employees but Burt found himself asking if it could wait a few days.

The agents came at four-thirty; Diaco called shortly after five.

"Sunday morning for breakfast?" Burt asked.

"Right," Diaco said.

"Ah, okay, the only thing is, is he gonna come?" Burt asked.

"Yes sir," Diaco said.

"I guess, you know, let's have it out of town," Burt said.

"How about right on Route 4, there, that Forum Diner?" Diaco suggested.

"The Forum Diner on Route 4?" Burt repeated out loud so

Pirog could react. When Pirog nodded affirmatively, Burt said fine.

They agreed on eleven o'clock. "Artie and I'll be there," Diaco said. "You can ask all the questions and we'll resolve everything right there."

"Okay," Burt said, "that's fair enough."

"Bye-bye," Diaco said.

That was it, short and sweet. Pirog told Burt to get to the FBI office on Sunday around nine because this would be a bigger operation and they would need more time to get ready. He gave Burt his home phone number in case anything came up, then left with O'Sullivan to begin making preparations.

As they drove back to the office together, Pirog and O'Sullivan talked about Diaco and Sutton, about how smoothly everything had gone so far. Mostly, though, they spoke of the intended "victim." Burt was unlike any informer they had ever encountered. Most of the others were criminals or society's misfits whose cooperation was usually reluctant or offered in return for some kind of protection.

What, they wondered, should they make of this young mayor who came to them voluntarily, pushed for the investigation, offered himself as a guinea pig and seemed far more sophisticated than the people who were pursuing him? Pirog and O'Sullivan considered all the questions but could find no answers. Soon they turned their attention to putting together the mechanics for the big day.

For his part Burt went home, grabbed a bite to eat and told Laurie about the unfolding drama. He had just begun to deal with the fear she was expressing when the phone rang. It was Kay Nest.

"That bastard!" she screamed into Burt's ear.

"What are you talking about?" Burt asked.

"Didn't you see it?" she said.

"See what?" Burt asked.

"Carl Stokes on NBC News," she shrieked. "He just said that if we win, the Sutton project will be approved."

"I don't believe you," Burt said. "He couldn't have said that."

He had.

On its evening news, WNBC-TV, the local affiliate in the metropolitan New York area, had done an item on the Wednesday night board of adjustment vote in Fort Lee. After showing a filmed report, Jim Hartz, the show's anchorman, turned to Carl Stokes, a former Mayor of Cleveland who was now doing a regular feature for the program called "Urban Journal."

"Now that you've watched this thing for the last three months," Hartz asked Stokes, "what do you think will happen?"

"Well, Jim, it is going to depend a great deal on the June 4 Democratic primary," Stokes said. "If the incumbent councilmen do win, I believe shortly after the election the builder will come in with a scaled-down model and they will push it through. If the insurgents happen to defeat the incumbents, then that structure will not be built. Just one thing you ought to know that our investigation has disclosed about the incumbent councilmen: We have found out that the builders, the contractors, the real estate developers around there have funneled some five thousand dollars to the incumbent councilmen through a committee—that then sent the money into these men. So you can clearly see they will be for the developers."

Burt got off the phone after getting the text and slumped in his chair. Friends and campaign workers started calling to say that Stokes must have had his material written for him by Serota. They urged Burt to hold a press conference, to point out that the money Stokes referred to had been for another campaign, that it had been five *hundred* dollars, not five thousand, and that the contributors had not included Sutton. What the hell did his project have to do with any of this, they asked. And why the hell hadn't Stokes interviewed Burt before airing his charge?

Burt listened to his supporters, but he drew no comfort from them. "I don't believe this," he kept saying. "It's like a nightmare."

To hold a press conference, he knew, would only make things worse. "By defending ourselves," he told one caller, "we just air the charges again. I'm telling you, there's not a damned thing we can do. Sampath will run the story under banner headlines. Serota's people are probably already at the printer. I think we have just lost the election."

Not even to his closest associates could Burt reveal that the Stokes report brought him pain for reasons that went beyond the election. But later that night, he did tell his father.

Dave Ross stopped in for some coffee, and when he asked his son how much developers had in fact contributed, Burt told him the whole story.

As the elder Ross heard about Diaco, Sutton, the U.S. Attorney and the FBI, his face became numb and his hands trembled. When Burt had finished, there was a long pause.

"I can only give you one piece of advice," Dave Ross finally said.

"What's that?" Burt asked.

"Don't tell your mother."

11

Saturday, May 25.

Still in a daze, Burt spent the morning driving kids around to deliver campaign literature. This week's flyer carried the headline, "Mammoth George Washington Shopping Mall Plan Defeated." Serota's side countered with "Fort Lee Is Becoming a Concrete Jungle."

When Burt told his workers to destroy any of Serota's literature they could find, a fourteen-year-old girl asked him if that wasn't unfair.

"Not at all," Burt said. "They do the same thing to us, and I'm sure you've learned in civics class that equality is a basic part of any democracy."

After lunch he went to Borough Hall where he had summoned fifteen dependable Greeks to divide the responsibility of getting out the Hellenic vote on Election Day. There were about a thousand Greek votes in town, a sizable bloc whose leaders Burt had carefully cultivated. The Greeks sat around a conference table as George Karageorge, the chunky owner of a local diner, read from the lists of voters. Karageorge sweated a lot and told jokes in an impish falsetto. And as he sat there yelling "Saponakis, who gonna take Saponakis?" Burt loved him.

Later in the afternoon Burt had an interview with a young woman who was writing an article on local zoning laws. The woman had a curious style: She would ask a question, look out the window while Burt answered, then smile enigmatically and ask, "You don't really believe that, do you?" It went like that for perhaps twenty minutes. Then she asked Burt if he believed in regional planning. When he said he did, she moved in for the kill.

"And exactly what have you done to help further it?" she asked.

"Absolutely nothing," Burt said.

"Why not?" she asked.

"Because I get paid five thousand dollars a year to be mayor," Burt said, "and it's a part-time job that I already spend forty hours or more a week at. That doesn't give me much leisure time."

The woman was not about to yield. "Well, what exactly do you do with your leisure time?" she asked.

Burt leaned across his desk, cocked his chin and whispered as if he were taking her into his confidence, "I spend my leisure time getting interviewed by dumb people."

Laurie joined him that night for dinner at the home of Mamma Gallo, an elderly woman who had invited him in for tortoni when he was knocking on doors during his own campaign. He had been coming back ever since. Mamma Gallo treated Burt like a son, worrying if he didn't eat enough of her *vitello tonnato*, plotting revenge against anyone who opposed him. Her skin felt like silk and her clear brown eyes would tear so much when she laughed that she would have to remove her glasses.

On this evening everyone was laughing. Mamma Gallo had recently been operated on, and as she described the medical outlook, Burt slapped his thigh with delight.

"The doctor, he say 'You should be able to live a normal life to at least seventy-five,' " Mamma Gallo said, "and I say 'That's a wonderful news, doctor, since I'm a now eighty-seven.' "

As they left, Burt reminded Mamma to be sure to vote.

"You think you gotta tell me that?" she said, feigning deep hurt. "You just worry about taking care of yourself. You no look a so good to me."

Sunday, May 26.

When the phone rang at eight, it felt like it had gone off in his stomach. Since Diaco had begun calling regularly, the ringing actually caused Burt physical pain.

It was Burt's father. Laurie had left early for ambulance duty and Burt had asked Dave Ross to wake him. He was so tired that he had been afraid he would sleep through the alarm. He was due at the FBI office at nine.

The fatigue disappeared quickly. It was like the fishing trips he went on in Canada each summer with his father. The wake-up call at the lodge would come at six, and Burt would roll over in bed and moan. Then he would realize where he was, that he was going out after big northern pike, and he would jump up in anticipation.

He dressed quickly, lit a cigar and was on the road by eight-thirty. It was a beautiful day. The early morning streets were deserted, and spring flowers softened the lines of the rectangular brick homes.

The FBI office Burt walked into on this Sunday of Memorial Day weekend bore no resemblance to the one he had first visited two days before. On Friday it had been nearly empty; today, it was like Allied command headquarters on the eve of D-Day.

When Burt arrived, Bernie Pirog was already briefing the

troops. He was sitting on a desk in the middle of the main room. Clustered around him were two dozen agents, getting directions to the Forum Diner, descriptions of Sutton and Diaco and a detailed run-down on the whole operation.

At one corner of the room four men were assembling electronic listening devices. In another area five men and a woman were fastening cameras to the insides of attache cases, shirt sleeves and a fishing rod case.

The whole scene reminded Burt of movies he had seen and thought implausible. Three of the agents around Pirog wore dungarees, plaid shirts and hats decorated with trout flies. A young couple had on tennis whites and sneakers. Several looked like middle-aged businessmen. Two matronly women in somber suits were carrying bibles. A few young men had moustaches and long hair.

As Pirog continued talking, Burt paced the room. He dealt with the tension in the only way he knew. He made wisecracks. At one point he heard Pirog refer to Sutton as "Trucker" and Diaco as "Trucker's Helper." Then he figured out that the "eyes" were the agents who would be in direct visual contact with him, the "ears" the ones who would be taping the meeting. "So what's my code name?" Burt said to no one in particular, "Pigeon?"

Shortly after ten Pirog began dispatching the agents in intervals of five minutes. As they made final checks of their guns and equipment, they exchanged small talk, like paratroopers before a combat jump. Burt envied them their camaraderie. The sensation that he was a character in a grade-B movie continued.

When Pirog turned to Burt, he explained that this time they would outfit him with a body transmitter. "It'll be better this way," he said. "We'll be able to hear you at all times and we can simultaneously tape the conversation."

"Are you going to tape from here?" Burt asked.

"No, it will be done closer to the diner," Pirog said.

Burt shook his head. "Don't tell me," he said, "that you're going to have a truck with an Ace Laundry sign parked outside."

Pirog smiled. "Ace Laundry is out of style, Burt," he said. "And besides, I don't think it's a good idea for you to know all the details. It will only disturb your concentration."

Another agent came over and asked the mayor to take off his shirt and lower his pants. He taped a transmitter the size of a cigarette pack to the inside of Burt's left buttock pocket. Then he punched a tiny hole in the pocket and ran a wire through it. He attached one end of the wire to the transmitter, the other to a microphone the size of a pencil eraser. He told Burt to zip up his pants and fasten his belt before securing the mike to the inside of the buckle.

"I can't believe this is strong enough to pick up everything," Burt said.

"Keep talking," the agent said, and he walked from the room.

Burt began chanting the Hebrew prayers he had learned for his Bar Mitzvah. A few moments later the agent returned, looked at him quizzically and said the equipment worked fine.

Turning now to the meeting itself, Burt expressed concern that if he said too much, he might be accused of entrapment.

"There are only two things you want to know from them," Pirog advised. "What they want you to do and why. Remember, they're the ones who want the meeting, so let them do the talking. Especially Sutton."

Burt was still unsure of himself. "But what do I do if they don't bring up money today?" he asked.

"They will," Pirog said. "They can't very well tell you what they want without saying what they're prepared to give."

Still another dark cloud crossed Burt's mind. "What if they want to give me the down payment today, and say I've got to go somewhere with them to get it? That scares the hell out of me. Maybe they've spotted something wrong. Maybe they want

114

to take me for a ride. I'm telling you, if Diaco smells a rat, I'm in big trouble."

Pirog told Burt that if they wanted him to go somewhere, he should try to get out of it. "But go if you have to," he said. "If you blow your cover now, we don't have a case, and then you're really vulnerable. And anyway, we have a helicopter standing by. You won't be out of our sight, I promise."

There was one last item on Burt's agenda. "Are you going to arrest these guys today or not?" he asked Pirog. "I can't take much more of this. It's not just the fear thing. It's also the double life I'm leading, trying to act normal with friends and relatives when all the while—"

Pirog put his arm gently on Burt's shoulder.

"I know what you're going through," he said. "Just believe me. I want this thing over as much as you do. Let's see how it plays out today. We'll move at the right time. There's no sense coming up short now."

Burt couldn't argue with that. He looked at his watch. It was ten forty-five. He had to go to the bathroom.

When he returned, he reached for his jacket and prepared to leave. Pirog told him to wait. "We'll be informed when they're at the diner," he said, "and I'd like them there before you go."

They didn't have to wait long. At five of eleven a voice came over the wall speaker: "Trucker and Trucker's Helper inside. Arrived separately, conferred in Trucker's car and entered building."

Pirog shook Burt's hand. "Don't drive straight back after the meeting," he said. "They may have someone on you. Weave around a little. And good luck."

Burt was just stepping into the elevator when Pirog dashed out after him.

"Jesus, I almost forgot," he said. "Let me see your wallet. If you happen to come back here with more money than when you left, we'll want a record of that."

He counted twenty dollars and change.

The Forum Diner is in Paramus, less than two miles west of the FBI office. It is hunched up against an overpass that straddles two huge department stores, a score of smaller shops and acres of parking lots. It was precisely this kind of shopping center that Fort Lee residents didn't want on their main street.

On Sundays when the stores are closed, business is light at the Forum. As Burt pulled into the parking lot, fewer than half of the two hundred spaces were full. Two women carrying bibles were just getting out of their car.

Diaco was waiting in the foyer. He motioned for Burt to follow and led him past a hostess in a black uniform to a corner table. Sutton was already seated. He moved over to make room for Burt, and Diaco sat across from them.

It was the first time Burt had been in the Forum. It was nothing like the kind of diner he had gone to as a kid. This place reminded him of a Howard Johnson's that had tried to step up in class by installing imitation marble tables and electric candles.

As he slid in next to Sutton and shook his hand, Burt got his first look at the developer in several months. He had a fresh tan and looked radiantly healthy.

"You understand why I wanted to meet with you, Arthur," Burt began. "This guy that I don't know from Adam comes to me and offers me a half million dollars, and with all due respect to Joey, he doesn't even know what you want. You know me well enough to come to me directly. You're a businessman. I'm a businessman. If you want me to take risks, you've got to take them too."

Sutton nodded but did not answer. The waitress had stopped at their table, and Sutton ordered scrambled eggs, well done.

When she left, Sutton lit a cigarette and looked around. He didn't seem happy to be there.

"I'm not saying we're both going down in the boat together," Burt said. "I don't want anyone to go down in the boat. I'm

116

not a moron. All I'm saying is that if ever I take the rope, ever . . ."

This was the kind of language Diaco understood. "I'm with you," he said.

Burt looked at Sutton, shook his head and smiled. "He says he's with me."

Sutton seemed anxious to get away from this kind of talk. He pulled a pen from his brown sports jacket and began drawing lines on a napkin. He spoke without looking at Burt.

"What we want is very simple," Sutton said. "We're going to come back in with a reduced plan. We're going down from three- to two-million square feet. We only need two variances now. We need the one- and two-family rezoned commercial and we need Hudson Street vacated. You can forget everything else."

Burt felt a warm flush go through him. The reduced plan that Sutton was willing to pay half a million dollars to get approved was not far from what the Mayor would have supported on its own merits.

He reached for his glass of water, took a slow drink and finally found something to say. "I told you many times that the project would be voted down, Arthur. It was just too big. Nobody would buy it. And one of the main problems is still going to be the traffic. You haven't solved that yet."

Sutton began drawing on the napkin again, mapping out alternate routes. Burt had stopped listening. He looked over at Sutton and the whole cops and robbers fantasy died. Diaco was different. Burt had never identified with him. But as he watched Sutton, he saw a man who was like a hundred other men he knew, middle-aged businessmen who loved their families, gave to charity, played golf on weekends and were proud of their big houses and cars. And Burt knew that when they had to, these men would pay off a buyer, fix up an out-of-town client with a whore, keep two sets of books. Maybe they even did it when it wasn't necessary. But they weren't bad men. Not really.

117

So as Burt looked at this fifty-two-year-old man with graying hair and a slight paunch who was sitting so close to him that their bodies touched, and as he listened to the sincere voice explain how the traffic problems could be overcome, he felt sadness. It wasn't Sutton. It was the whole lousy system. They were all part of it, and only circumstance would now make it seem otherwise. He wanted to lean over and whisper, "Arthur, get the hell out of here."

Of course it was too late. The roles had been cast. Burt slowly moved his eyes around. There were agents everywhere.

Sutton put down his pen and turned to Burt. He said the critical factor now was the timing. "I've got a June 15 deadline, and the banks are ready to strangle me."

Burt couldn't believe what Sutton was saying. God himself could not get the board of adjustment to reconvene, hold hearings and approve the variances in less than three weeks. Sutton was either incredibly stupid or under such pressure that he could no longer think rationally.

"What you're asking me to do is awfully difficult," Burt said. "The board of adjustment is tired. They've just finished all those hearings on your application, Arthur, and there are others that have just been sitting there. Two months would be one thing, but three weeks, I just don't . . ."

"You can do it," Diaco cut in like a football coach giving his team a pep talk. "You can do it."

"Two months is no good," Sutton said. "It might as well be two years. We need it now."

For the first time, Burt became aware of a constant tic under Sutton's left eye.

"I wish I could be as certain as Joey," Burt said. "You know, Serota is spending tens of thousands of dollars to knock my block off. I don't . . ."

"Wait, wait, wait a minute," Sutton said.

"His whole thing seems to be against us and he may win," Burt continued.

"Against what?" Sutton asked.

"This project," Burt said.

Sutton turned angrily to Diaco. "Look, Joey," he said, "I'm gonna tell you, Serota is your problem, all right? And Serota better not object to anything."

"I told you," Diaco said, "there won't be any problems."

Diaco wouldn't say any more, but it was enough to get Burt's juices flowing again.

"Look, Arthur," he said, "You're asking me to do an awful lot of work in the next three weeks."

For the first time, Sutton looked directly at him. "Yes," he said, "you'll be working for me twenty-four hours a day."

Now Burt had his opening, an approach that could be made without the slightest risk of entrapment.

"Why should I be working for you twenty-four hours a day, Arthur?" he asked.

Diaco looked exasperated. "Because we're gonna give you half a million dollars," he said.

There it was, but it was coming from the wrong person.

"When?" Burt asked. Now Sutton took over.

"Very soon, Burt," he said. "Very soon."

"How much in cash?" Burt asked.

"Two hundred," Sutton said. "A hundred soon and a hundred when it's approved. I'd like to give you the other three in some kind of real estate. Real estate has a lot of advantages. There's going to be a McDonald's in the shopping center, and we can give you a piece of that."

Burt's sympathy for Sutton was evaporating. "This guy is a crook," he kept telling himself. "He's just as bad as Diaco, maybe worse. At least Diaco doesn't pretend to be anything else. But Sutton cloaks himself in respectability, uses Diaco as a stalking horse and doesn't come out until he thinks it's safe. Fuck him."

Sutton started to say something, but Burt cut him off with a nudge in the side. "Take it easy, Arthur," he said, pointing to the waitress who was walking past the table. "The whole world doesn't have to know what we're talking about."

There didn't seem to be much more to say anyway. They had finished eating, and as Diaco leaned across the table to light Burt's cigar, he again stressed the importance of getting speedy action by the board of adjustment.

"Well," Burt said, "I have just one more question. If you're going to give me the money soon, what do I do with it if I can't make your deadline?"

In fact, Burt couldn't deliver if he wanted to, but when he put the question to them, Sutton only shrugged knowingly and said, "Well, maybe it would be a good idea if you didn't spend the first hundred right away."

Diaco turned to Burt and smiled. "Don't listen to that, Burt," he said. "You go right ahead and spend it."

As though by prearranged signal, Sutton and Diaco then rose to their feet. "Arthur and I are going to the men's room," Diaco said. "We'll be right back."

Burt stood up so Sutton could get out and watched the two men walk away. For the first time he was able to look around freely. The fishermen were sitting closest to him. He tried to make eye contact. They didn't respond.

Suddenly it hit him. He was going to get the money today. Why the hell else would they have gone to the men's room if not to finalize it?

Burt sat down slowly and put his elbows on the table and his chin in his hands. Looking down, he spoke almost inaudibly. "They're meeting in the men's room. I think they're going to give me the money now." He repeated it three times.

Sutton and Diaco returned in a few minutes, and Burt moved over to the window seat. As Sutton sidled next to him, he patted Burt on the side. The mayor froze. Sutton touched him exactly where the cassette was strapped. Two or three seconds passed before Burt remembered: He wasn't wearing the cassette today. Thank God they had switched to the transmitter.

"Okay, Burt," Diaco said, "we're going to give you the money now."

Burt's pulse quickened. "I don't want it in big bills," he said.

"Don't worry," Sutton said, his voice breaking slightly, "it's all in small bills. Tens, twenties and thirties."

Burt relaxed. "Listen, brother," he laughed, "if you're going to give it to me in tens, twenties and thirties, I don't want to do business."

Sutton shook his head. "Christ," he muttered, "did I really say that?"

Still nodding, Sutton stood up and reached for his coat. "All right," he said, "I'm going to leave you gentlemen. Bye-bye."

"Shit!" Burt thought as Sutton walked away. "The bastard is leaving the dirty work to his assistant. They better have enough on him already."

He turned to Diaco. "I hope we don't have to go far," he said. "It's already past twelve, and I've got an appointment at one."

"Relax," Diaco said. "It's not far away."

"Fine," Burt said. "I'll be back in a second. I've got to take a leak."

The mayor walked into the men's room and looked under the stalls. No one was there. He approached the urinal, unzipped his fly, took out his penis, and looking down at it, whispered, "He's going to give me the money now. Jesus, I hope you can hear me."

To the agent who was wearing earphones in an electric appliance van parked across the street, the mayor sounded like he had taken cover behind a waterfall.

When Burt came out of the men's room, Diaco was gone. The waitress said the bill had been paid. Had something gone wrong?

The doubt didn't last long. As Burt stepped outside, Diaco was pulling up in his Continental. He motioned for Burt to get in, then drove toward the parking lot exit. Burt began to panic, but at the last moment, Diaco swerved around and pulled into a space far away from any other cars.

Without speaking, he turned off the ignition, reached under his seat and pulled out a brown attache case. He opened it and took out a purple accordian folder. Untying the strings, he opened the folder and put it on the seat so Burt could look inside.

It was filled with cash. Neatly stacked packets of tens, twenties and fifties. The money was so new and crisp that it seemed unreal.

"Is it a hundred?" Burt asked.

Diaco chuckled. "On the button," he said. "Want to count it?"

Burt didn't want to touch the money before the FBI had gone through it. "I'm sure it's right," he said. "You'll hear from me if it isn't."

Diaco closed the folder, tied it shut and started the engine. He drove to Burt's car, stopped and put the folder on the mayor's lap.

"Okay, Burt," he said. "I'll be talking to you. If you need me, you know where to get hold of me, right?"

"I won't call you 'til Tuesday," Burt said.

"If you need me during the day," Diaco said, "just leave your name and I'll reach out for you. Just say Burt."

As he walked the few feet to his car, Burt's hands trembled and he was afraid he'd drop the folder.

"Don't blow it now," he kept saying to himself.

He opened the trunk of his car. Inside, he saw the shopping bag he had used the day before to carry the flyers with the headline "Mammoth George Washington Shopping Mall Plan Defeated."

He put the folder in the shopping bag, closed the trunk and walked to his door. He could hear Diaco's car pull away, but he did not look back. He started his engine, drove to the overpass and headed east.

It had taken Burt only five minutes to drive from the FBI office to the Forum. It took him three times as long to make the return trip. He got on and off the highway, took side streets and kept looking through his rearview mirror. And as he drove, he sang, repeating the same lyrics over and over:

"We're in the money.
We're in the money."

By now, he thought, Sutton and Diaco must have been nabbed. He could almost see Diaco snarling as he was led away. Sutton would be different. Burt pictured him pulling into the long driveway of his estate and collapsing as agents sprang from the bushes. It was a much more vivid image.

It was almost one when Burt pulled up the parking ramp to the same spot he had gone to on Friday. This time, Pirog and half a dozen other agents were already there waiting.

Burt got out, opened the trunk and handed the shopping bag to Pirog.

"Did you hear everything?" he asked.

"Yes," Pirog said laughing. "Even your singing."

"I'm glad you enjoyed the performance," Burt said, "but what the hell is going on? Did you get them?"

"No," Pirog said. "Not yet."

"Why the hell not?" Burt exploded.

"Now take it easy," Pirog said. "Just take it easy. We want to check out the money first and make sure the tapes came out well. Relax a little, You were terrific."

Pirog and the others seemed so happy that Burt did begin to unwind. It occurred to him that Pirog must have known all along that there would be no immediate arrests but hadn't said anything because it might have made Burt more nervous. And as Burt thought about it, he knew Pirog had been right. But his part was over now, anyway. As they walked inside and agents patted him on the back and slapped his hand, Burt felt like a winning pitcher being mobbed by his teammates after a clutch performance.

Upstairs, the other agents began filing in. Each one told Burt

123

how great he had been. "You were a real pro," one of them said, which was the highest compliment of all.

Pirog handed out rubber gloves to four agents, who applied talcum powder to their hands before putting them on.

"I'll bet you a buck it's short," one of them said as he started to count. "They always try to screw you out of a few hundred."

Burt took the bet. An hour later he collected. It was, as Diaco had said, a hundred grand on the button. "I'm glad," Burt laughed as he put the dollar bill in his pocket, "that at least I'm coming away from this with something."

While the agents recounted and Burt took off his pants so the transmitter could be dismantled, Pirog called Bruce Goldstein at his home. After giving him a report, he handed the phone to Burt.

"Good job," the assistant U.S. Attorney told the mayor. "It sounds very good."

"Thank you, cousin Brucie," Burt said. "I'm glad you approve. Now perhaps you'd like to tell me when the hell you're going to bust these guys."

Goldstein repeated what Pirog had said. He wanted to fly the money to Washington to check out the serial numbers first, and he wanted to transcribe the tapes. This would take a couple of days because the secretaries were all off for the three-day weekend. Why didn't Burt come into his office on Tuesday so they could go over everything?

Without thinking, Burt answered in his Amos and Andy dialect. "Ahd be deelited to have de pleshuh of yaw company," he said, "but ah is jest a little confused heah. De way ah understands it, you is sittin right now wit de habeus corpsus. And what ah is afraid of is dat unless you arrests de habeus, ah is gonna end up de corpsus."

Goldstein laughed uncomfortably and told Burt not to worry. "There's no big rush," he said. "We'll move at the right time."

Burt was losing patience with other people's timetables. "Listen, Bruce," he said, "I've just been given a hundred thousand dollars by two men who expect a return on their investment. They want action in less than three weeks. They're going to be back to me soon, wanting to know what I'm doing. And I'll have nothing to say. Keep that in mind when you decide how much of a rush there is, will you?"

As Burt hung up and prepared to leave, Pirog handed him a slip of paper. It was a receipt for $100,000.

"Is this some kind of a joke?" Burt asked.

"Not at all," Pirog said. "It's standard procedure in cases like this. The money will eventually go to the government, but right now it's technically yours."

Burt took off his right shoe, put the receipt under the lift that helped support his bad leg and left. It was all over now but the headlines. And for the first time it occurred to him that those headlines could come before the election.

It was past two when he got home. He was coming down fast. The excitement was gone, and all that was left were exhaustion and raw nerves.

Laurie was sitting on the couch when he walked in. "How did it go?" she asked.

"Everything was perfect," Burt said as he reached for the phone to call his father. "They gave me the money. They're going to be arrested. It couldn't have been better."

When Burt put down the receiver, he saw tears running down Laurie's cheeks. He walked over and put his arms around her. "Is it because you were worrying?" he asked.

"I was worrying," Laurie sobbed, "but that's not it. Burt, I saw a man die this morning."

It took her several minutes to get the story out. While she had been on ambulance duty, an elderly man had collapsed from a heart attack. He had died on the way to the hospital. It was the first time Laurie had witnessed death. She was overcome with grief, anger and a vague sense of guilt. Burt offered some words of comfort, but he was confused. He had thought she was upset because of him. He was disappointed that she wasn't.

One of Laurie's Greek cousins was marrying a Puerto Rican later that afternoon about thirty miles away. The party was filled with drunken merriment, but Burt and Laurie sat quietly to one side, forcing an occasional smile, alone with their separate thoughts.

On the way home Burt's driving was erratic. Once he bounced off a side rail on the New Jersey Turnpike and nearly lost control of the car.

When they got to their lobby, Laurie's parents were waiting. As they entered the elevator together and began the trip up, Laurie turned to Burt and spoke for the first time in an hour.

"You know," she said, "it's getting so I don't feel safe in a car with you anymore."

Burt's face reddened and his fists clenched. "Will you shut your fucking mouth," he screamed. "Will you shut your mouth before I knock your teeth out." Now it was Burt who was sobbing. "If you're so concerned about my driving, drive yourself. I don't care who drives. Do you understand that?"

With Laurie's parents standing there frozen and uncomprehending, Burt reached into his pocket, pulled out the car keys and threw them at his wife.

The family dinner that they had looked forward to for weeks was like a wake. They were joined by Laurie's brother and his girl friend, both followers of the Guru Maharaj Ji and neither big on small talk. The Millers didn't know what was going on and they didn't ask. They had always sided with their son-in-law. So when Laurie came out of the kitchen with drinks, Joanne Miller lit into her daughter.

"What the hell are you doing to Burt?" she began. She got no further.

Laurie screamed "Oh, no," threw the ice bucket to the floor and ran from the apartment. Her brother and his girl friend ran after her, laid on some cosmic soothing and persuaded her to return. Everyone ate without speaking. The guests left before dessert.

Burt and Laurie said no more to each other. At ten, they both got into bed, turned in opposite directions and went to sleep. They were one week away from their first anniversary.

12

Roy Sampath was on the street delivering copies of *The Independent*. A banner headline heralded the Carl Stokes expose. Serota's candidates were working apartment lobbies, making sure everyone knew that the mayor and his candidates would support Sutton's project if they won. Councilwoman Pearl Moskowitz was preparing a letter to tell the town that, as an opponent of high rise development, she "wholeheartedly supported" Serota's candidates.

Burt and Laurie spent the morning making love and making up. The mayor's spirits had picked up considerably since last night. It was beginning to sink in that his meetings with Sutton and Diaco were over. And with the money already passed, it seemed inconceivable that arrests would not take place soon.

That night, Burt and Laurie went to see "The Sting." There was a scene in the film in which an attaché case was opened, revealing bundles of cash. As the audience whistled with delight, Burt nudged Laurie and whispered, "That ain't nothing, Poops."

Tuesday, May 28.

Burt drove to Newark early for his appointment with Bruce. Dick Shapiro and two other assistant U.S. Attorneys joined them. In one short week, everything had changed. The mayor was for real now. The evidence was in hand. The questions were friendly. There was laughter.

For nearly three hours they went over every detail of Sunday's meeting. When they had finished, Burt turned to Bruce and asked again when the arrests would be made.

"Don't concern yourself with that," Bruce said. "We know what we're doing."

"I know," Burt said, "but after everything that's happened, I think it would be tragic if this came out after the election and Serota's people won."

Bruce's answer sounded like a recorded announcement that had been made for just such occasions. It went something like this: "The United States Attorney's Office will not in any way permit the timing of an election to influence its own decision as to whether or when to prosecute a case." Turned away at the front door, Burt tried a side entrance. "Well, what am I supposed to do if in the meantime, Diaco gets to me and wants to meet?" he asked. "I'll tell you right now, that's something I'm not going to do."

Bruce smiled and said not to worry about it. There was something cryptic about his tone. It convinced Burt that arrests or indictments were imminent.

One nagging thought remained. Burt wanted to make sure that when the story broke, no one would conclude that he had considered taking the bribe and then gotten cold feet and turned informer. Bruce told Burt to relax. He asked him to come in for a few minutes the next morning so they could go over some final items.

Wednesday, May 29.

The cast was the same, but today the questions Bruce asked dealt exclusively with all the phone calls Diaco had made to Burt. Bruce asked over and over where Burt and Diaco had been during these calls, and the mayor was confused about the reason for this game of twenty questions. Then it registered. The U.S. Attorney's Office was concerned with jurisdiction. Unless Burt and Diaco had been in different states during at least one of these calls, there would be no basis for federal charges. And this was clearly not a case that the U.S. Attorney would want to hand over to a state prosecutor.

Burt wasn't much help. He knew where *he* had been at all times, but not where Diaco had called from. So when Bruce suggested that the FBI tap Burt's office phone in the event that Diaco called again, Burt readily agreed. If this was all that was holding up the action, he wanted to close the loophole as soon as possible.

Permission for the FBI to tap his phone was quickly granted by L.F. Rothschild and the New York Stock Exchange. That afternoon, two agents met Burt at his office to set it up. The other brokers looked on quizzically as the tape recorder and suction cup were attached, but Burt volunteered no information and the presence of two strangers was enough to keep them from asking questions. There was no assurance that Diaco would call Burt at his office, but it seemed likely since the mayor hadn't gotten back to him yet. The only question was when.

The answer came in less than an hour. Burt's phone rang and his secretary Millie told him Mr. DiGiacomo was on the line.

"Good afternoon," Diaco said cheerfully. "You're busier than a beaver."

"Well, you know this is campaign time," Burt said. "I'm at the printer's half the day."

"Yeah, I know," Diaco said. "What's his name, Art, tried to get hold of me, okay. He wanted me to talk to you in regard to

130

possibly putting something in that's within the variance, where you don't need a change or anything, just so he can log it in because of his problems with the bank."

"Yeah, I can understand that," Burt said. "Can you do me a favor? I got someone here who's going to buy some bonds from me and, you know, I have to do a little business."

"Okay," Diaco said, "I'll call you back."

"Are you at the four–eight–four number?" Burt asked.

"No, no, I'm down in south Jersey," Diaco said.

"You're in south Jersey?" Burt repeated. "Okay, call me back in about fifteen minutes."

"All right, fine," Diaco said. "Sell, sell, sell."

"No," Burt said. "Buy."

Diaco laughed. "Buy," he said.

Burt nodded to the agents when he got off. Now they had everything, jurisdiction and all.

When Diaco called back twenty minutes later and suggested that Burt meet him and Sutton for dinner the following night, Burt agreed. He knew that this was one engagement he wouldn't have to keep.

"Where the hell am I gonna take ya?" Diaco asked. "How about the same diner?"

"Okay," Burt said, "but you're cheap."

Diaco laughed. "No, no," he said. "That's no problem, but I'm looking for a place to go out that way."

"If you want the diner, the diner it is," Burt said. "It's all right."

When he had finished, Burt called Bruce to tell him that Diaco had called from New Jersey. He also told Bruce about the dinner arrangement, but he put him on notice. "I hope you understand," he said, "that I'm not going to that meeting."

"I understand," Bruce said. "Look, Jonathan is back from vacation, so why don't you come in first thing in the morning and be prepared to spend some time here."

That was the tip-off. Indictments were coming the next day.

Since Bruce didn't expect him to attend the dinner and wanted him in Newark in the morning, Burt could read between the lines: He would appear before a grand jury and indictments would swiftly follow. The return of U.S. Attorney Jonathan Goldstein added to Burt's confidence. The election was six days away. If he had written the script himself, the timing couldn't have been better.

Thursday, May 30.

As Burt put on a gray suit and conservative tie and left for Newark, Laurie and her father-in-law discussed the best way to break the news to Rose Ross. Burt's mother had a minor heart ailment and her husband, remembering how he had trembled when he first heard the story, wanted to tell his wife as gently as possible. No talk about organized crime or the FBI, he suggested. Just give her a sugar-coated version and keep her away from newspapers and television.

As they sat together at the elder Rosses' kitchen table, Dave clapped his hands in feigned glee and forced an unconvincing laugh. "Rose," he said, "I want you to prepare yourself because I have some wonderful news that's going to make you very proud. A few hours from now your son is going to be a hero. We didn't want to tell you before, but Burt was offered a half-million-dollar bribe by some real estate people, and he worked with the U.S. Attorney's Office, and they're going to be arrested today. Burt's in Newark now. By this afternoon the whole story should be out."

Rose Ross had taken enough of her husband's medicine during their marriage to know when she was being fed a placebo. So, as he spoke, her eyes widened and her mouth dropped open. Then she rose slowly to her feet and the tears rolled down her cheeks. Her husband, too, broke down and the two of them embraced.

132

In Newark, Burt waited impatiently to be taken in to see the boss. He had met Jonathan Goldstein once or twice before and had been thoroughly impressed. At thirty-three, Jonathan was the youngest U.S. Attorney in the country and probably the most aggressive. After New York University Law School he had gone directly into the Justice Department's division of organized crime and racketeering. Interrupted only by a hitch as a captain with an Army intelligence unit in Thailand, he had been sending people to jail ever since. He was tall and sandy-haired, his style somber, low-key and careful. What warmth he showed toward people like Burt seemed calculated to elicit whatever cooperation he was looking for at the moment.

These were all qualities the mayor could relate to, but what affected him most about Jonathan was his stutter. Burt identified with people who had overcome handicaps. He admired a man who could take his stutter into crowded courtrooms and speak so well on behalf of the United States. The U.S. Attorney's success came not from impassioned eloquence, but from raw intelligence and dedicated effort. In fact it seemed that his work was his life. The vacation he had just come back from with his wife and two sons was his first in five years.

When Burt was ushered to his office, he found Bruce Goldstein, Dick Shapiro and two other assistants, John Barry and Dick Hellstern, already there.

Jonathan shook his hand warmly. "I've been going over everything," he said. "You were just great. We have practically everything we need now."

Perhaps it was the word "practically," or that Jonathan's associates seemed to be looking at him apprehensively, but Burt began to perspire.

"Am I going before a grand jury today or not?" he demanded.

"Calm down," Jonathan said. "We're almost there. We just need—"

"Wait a minute," Burt shouted. "There is no way that I'm going to that meeting tonight. If that's what's on your mind, you can just forget it. I've had it. You can get yourself another pigeon."

Jonathan looked directly at Burt. His voice was subdued. "There is no way we can force you to go," he said. "It's completely your decision to make. I know what you've been through. I can only tell you that the tape of Sunday's meeting is still being analyzed, and we want to fly a sound expert up from Washington so that we get it right this time."

"Are you telling me the Sunday tape didn't come out?" Burt asked.

"I'm not telling you anything," Jonathan said, "except that it would be extremely helpful if you were to attend that dinner."

As the five prosecutors waited for his response, a distant memory surfaced in Burt's mind. He was seven years old, had been in the hospital for four months and was happily preparing to leave. The day before his planned departure, his parents told him that the doctors had changed their minds and wanted him to stay for another two months. It was up to him to make the decision, they said. Burt wanted to cry. But if it was the right thing, how could he argue? He had stayed.

Now, Burt looked around and realized that he had no choice. "All right, I'll do it," he said, "but after this, get yourself someone else."

Jonathan extended his hand. "You've done so well up to now that one more meeting shouldn't be any problem," he said. "In fact, my only advice is that you not enjoy yourself so much that you make any more jokes or sing songs like 'We're In the Money.' "

Burt left Newark a very unhappy man. To the relatives who were waiting anxiously in Fort Lee, he brought heartache instead of headlines. He just couldn't believe, he said, that he would be able to get his adrenalin going again.

Later that afternoon, Diaco called to switch the restaurant from the Forum to the Red Coach Grill, ten miles to the west.

He didn't like being called cheap. Seven would be a good time.

Burt cleared the place with Bernie Pirog and drove to the FBI office at five. The scene was identical to Sunday's except that all the faces had changed. To avoid any possibility that Sutton and Diaco might recognize someone from Sunday, Pirog had brought in a new crew of twenty agents. And because the restaurant had been stepped up in class, he had told everyone to dress accordingly. This time there were no fishermen or jeans —just a group of inconspicuous businessmen, a few with their wives.

Pirog reassured Burt that everything would be all right, that the place would be covered inside and out. Burt puffed nervously on his cigar and kept saying, "This is it for me. I'm not going through this anymore."

At five-thirty the sound expert came in from the airport. He was a small man with close-cropped white hair. It was clear from the confident way he worked that he was a master of his trade. Within minutes he had attached a transmitter to Burt's chest with tape and suction cups and placed a tiny mike underneath his tie. Once again Burt would be transmitting live and would be simultaneously taped. Once again Pirog told him to find out what Sutton wanted him to do and why. "And see if you can't learn anything about anyone else," he said.

The agents began leaving at six. Burt was on the road forty minutes later. Halfway to Saddle Brook, a car pulled alongside him and honked. Burt jumped slightly at the wheel, then recognized the driver as a Fort Lee tenant leader. His nerves were so raw by this time that he worried whether he could get through this meeting without making some big mistake.

Sutton was standing in front of the Red Coach smoking a cigarette as Burt arrived. The two shook hands, walked in together and were ushered to a booth. Burt lit another cigar and glanced around. The restaurant was candlelit. Soft music floated through the room. Sitting in the next booth, separated from

Burt's by a thin panel of translucent plastic, were four agents. On the floor next to one of them was an attaché case that held the recording equipment.

Burt was anxious to get it all out quickly. "Before Joey gets here, let me understand one thing," he began, "because he gets me a little confused. Now the date you need this done is what?"

Sutton said he'd like to reapply right after the election and get final approval within two weeks. It would have been a physical impossibility under any conditions, but Burt was in no mood to discuss timing now. He nodded his head and moved on.

"There is something else that I get a little confused about," he said. "I'm glad I can talk about it with you, okay. You gave me the hundred thousand on well, whatever. When do I get the other four hundred?"

"Okay, here's what I want to do," Sutton said. "I'd like to give you two hundred the night it passes."

"In cash?" Burt asked.

"In cash," Sutton said. "Same thing, you know, tens and twenties, no tens and thirties." He laughed. "Okay, I wasn't thinking that day."

"Took me hours to count it," Burt said.

"We'd like to give you another two in cash," Sutton continued, "and then what I'd like to do, I'd like to work out anything you want. You know, cash is a murderous problem. If we have time, we can make it all cash. If you give me six months, I can pull it down, 'cause you know, everybody's watching everybody . . ."

They hadn't been there ten minutes, and already Burt had gotten what he came for. What the hell would he talk about for the next hour, he wondered.

"All right," he said. "Time is not such a problem. I'm youngish."

"Yeah, me too," Sutton said.

"How old are you, Art?" Burt asked.

"Guess," Sutton said.

"Around fifty," Burt said.

"You're pretty close," Sutton said. "Fifty-two. I've been a developer since I got out of the Marine Corps, I've been a developer since 1946. I've done about a billion dollars' worth of construction in New York, California and Indiana."

"In '46 I was three years old," Burt said. "When the hell did you meet this Joey guy?"

"Let me tell you," Sutton began. "There was a—hey, here he is."

Diaco sat down next to Sutton and shook his head. "I asked this guy if anybody was waiting for me," he muttered. "He said no. I been waiting outside for ten minutes."

"I don't care what happens," Sutton said, "but the next meeting we got to make it Club C——— in New York. It's the wildest place. I never went to a club in my life where you go to the bar and fifteen broads line up."

"You know, I lost my pipe," Burt said. "I had a real good pipe. I must have left it at the damn diner."

Diaco smiled. "You must have got nervous and dropped it on the way out," he said. "Sure it didn't fall in the trunk?"

"These guys are burying themselves," Burt thought.

"You're gonna get a charge out of this, Artie," Diaco went on. He told Sutton how Burt had called him cheap for wanting to eat at the Forum again. The developer said there was a better reason for not eating there: "Thursday night is shopping center night, and everybody in Fort Lee goes there," he said.

Sutton seemed much more at ease than he had been on Sunday. He took Burt into his confidence by telling him about some of the early problems he had getting his friend Tony Cutrupi excavation work in Fort Lee. "I told this guy, I have a debt because Cutrupi is a personal friend of mine," he said. "We go out together, our wives play cards together and I like the guy personally."

"You gotta respect that," Diaco said.

Burt's Bloody Mary was starting to take effect. For the first time, he felt relaxed. For twenty minutes he quizzed Sutton on the basics of construction, and the developer eagerly explained how excavation worked, how blasting was done, how foundations were laid and concrete mixed. As Sutton talked, Burt briefly forgot that he was in a restaurant laying his own foundation, for the developer's arrest.

"Now the idea of concrete, Burt, is you take your sand and your stone, and you put this paste, which is cement, around it, and the stone has to stay equally distributed," Sutton said as he described the problems of bridge building. "The stone is heavy. Now you pour your concrete on a bridge, and there's a twenty-ton truck going by and it hits that steel beam that supports the concrete and it keeps hitting it and every time it vibrates, the stone, which is the heaviest material, goes down and the cement comes up and the damn thing isn't worth the trouble."

Burt didn't understand a thing Sutton was saying. He understood even less when Diaco piped in to give him a course in electrical wiring. Still, he didn't want to seem dumb, so he nodded his head frequently.

Sutton and Diaco had gotten their steak sandwiches, and Burt was into his clam chowder and diet salad. As the three ate, Sutton told Diaco how Burt was to be paid.

Diaco didn't like the cash setup. "Five will cost you seven," he told Sutton. "You're forgetting the mathematics. Who the fuck is going to pay me to transpose it?"

"You know what he's saying," Sutton explained to Burt. "In order for me to transpose—let me interpret—to transpose the five into cash would cost me like seven. This is what he's saying, but what I'm saying is, if we have the element of time, the easier it is for me."

The solution, Sutton suggested, would be for Burt to get paid off in smaller amounts, like $20,000 a month. "If he can wait and gives us the time," he said to Diaco, "we'll turn it all into green."

Burt said that would be fine, as long as there was no reduction in the price and he didn't have too much contact with Sutton.

"I don't want to meet you every day," he said.

"Okay, that settles that," Sutton said, turning to Diaco. "He's already got a hundred in his hands. I already gave it to him, right?"

"You gotta talk with Andy on that," Diaco said, "but there's no problem. Whatever we agreed to him, he's gonna get."

Burt didn't know who Andy was, but he sensed that he had something to do with laundering dirty money, and that there was a price for his service. He pressed for more information.

"What concerns me," he told Sutton, "is he says the three of us. Now, all of a sudden we got a new guy, Andy. How does he get into the picture?"

"It's a mechanical thing," Diaco said.

"There's nobody involved," Sutton said, covering his slip. "There's one, two, three. There's nobody else. Just let it stand."

Diaco was just as eager to change the conversation. "I'll tell you," he said to Burt. "These deals don't come off so easy. You're learning something. They take a lot of guts, loving, dealing. And everybody you're dealing with is where you have faith in the guy, and I'm not just talking in general. Where you have faith, you do what you're supposed to and you don't have to go fighting."

Burt was really warming up now. Hopeful that he could get something more, he asked whether Serota was financing Roy Sampath's weekly, *The Independent*.

"You can't throw fuel on the fire," Diaco advised. "You just have to let it go because today's papers are yesterday's fish table cloth."

"Can't you give me any clues to who's behind that goddamn paper?" Burt persisted. "I'd give you fifty or the hundred back for that. I mean, I hate the guy."

"You can't control him," Diaco said. "He don't listen to anyone."

"That guy's lost seventy thousand dollars," Burt said. "Now who is giving him that money?"

139

"If it's not Serota, nobody is," Diaco said.

"You think Serota's giving him some?" Burt asked.

"Yeah, Serota's got to be," Sutton said. "Who else got the money? You know nobody else has got the money."

When he was a kid, Burt used to play a game at Passover called "Find the Matzoh." According to the rules of that game, he had been warm with Sampath. With Serota he was hot.

"What's Serota's role in here?" he asked Sutton. "What's his interest?"

"You know, I'll tell you," Sutton said. "I thought, honest to God, I thought Serota was looking for an interest. We have two mutual friends and I didn't go to Serota myself. I sent the guy in to feel him out. I was just curious to see. No way he is looking to touch this deal. He wants to get those people in, he's just there for the town. How do I know what he's doing? I just mind my own business."

Sutton seemed to be evasive. The bemused expression that Diaco had taken on made Burt unwilling to drop the subject.

"Why do you think you can control Serota if they win?" he asked Diaco. "That's the point."

Diaco glanced at Sutton, then turned to Burt. "I got a pretty good handle on him," he said. "Don't even think about it. No maybe. I'm telling you, he's guaranteed he's not going to give us one bit of nothing. . . . You know, really, you can tell somebody what you want and unless you really own the guy, okay, you know, he'll listen, he'll do what he can, but behind the scenes he's gonna do what his own makeup tells him to do. Right, Artie? But I'm saying we got the situation under hands where you're not going to get any black eyes, and that prick is not going to write any more things about this plaza."

Once again Diaco wasn't being very specific, Burt decided to let it go.

"I got a meeting tonight, a meeting tomorrow night," he said. "I'm just ready to go to bed."

"There is nothing left to fight anymore," Diaco said.

"I'm just tired," Burt said. "Tired of being mayor."

"Don't be tired of being mayor for a couple of years, will you please," Sutton said.

"You mean I'm not allowed to resign within the next week?" Burt laughed.

"You leave, I leave with you, kid," Sutton said.

"You get a refund," Burt said.

"Keep the refund and stick it in your ear," Sutton said. "Just don't leave me."

"Took me four hours to count it," Burt said. "I'm not going to stick it in my ear. . . . I want to go fishing around this time, go up to Canada. What do you do for relaxation?"

"I go over to Palm Springs," Sutton said. "I go up to northern California. I got a lot of property up there."

"You buy the land and build?" Burt asked. "Now you don't pour all the money into it. I mean that's ridiculous. Isn't interest terrible now?"

"In Florida, paid sixteen percent for money," Sutton said.

Diaco shook his head. "Crazy," he said.

Burt saw another opening. "So who's Investors Funding and what's wrong with them?" he asked. "Because they're down to about a dollar a share."

"Well, they backed a couple of losers," Sutton said. "They'll come up."

"I thought they owned some property in town," Burt said. "Matter of fact, they came to a planning board meeting recently."

"I know," Sutton said. "I sent them."

"And they just have loans?" Burt asked.

"They charge high interest rates," Sutton said. "They charge you in and they charge you out. This is what they'll do with me. First of all, the high interest rate—when I finally take them out, in the final deal, we'll give them a kicker, we'll give them five percent equity, something like that."

For the first time, Sutton had acknowledged a relationship

with Investors Funding, but although Burt would have liked to know more about the huge corporation, he did not pursue it directly.

"What made you decide on that piece of land in Fort Lee?" he asked. "I saw it six or eight years ago, and I said 'What a piece of land.'"

Sutton said that originally he had only wanted to buy part of the seventeen acres to build a headquarters for a chemical company. But as other companies expressed interest in relocating to the site, the project mushroomed and he had trouble buying individual parcels from all the small property owners.

"An old guy, nice fellow, we sit down, we say we'd like to buy the piece," Sutton said. "He says it's not for sale. You want to lease it, I want eight thousand dollars a year. I say you got it. The old guy, he says I've been reconsidering. I want ten thousand. I says, well, okay, let's draw up the papers and we'll give you the ten. He says I want twelve. I says what are you doing here, playing games? I walk out the door. He calls me up, he says I thought it over and I'll tell you what. I'll take fourteen. . . . Now I go into some antique shop, I go in to buy, the guy greets me with both arms, puts his arms around me. Boom, twenty thousand dollars you own the piece. I says this is more like it, right? So I go next door, there's a woman. . . . She's got a pair out like this. So I said to her, I said I'd like to buy your land. She said sure, you and forty other guys, and boom, closed the door in my face. Now I start going around, you know, move around."

The waitress interrupted them and Sutton ended the monologue. He paid the check, then turned to Burt. "The only thing is," he said, "we'll come in on the fourteenth."

"I understand that already," Burt said.

"Okay?" Sutton asked.

"No problem," Burt said.

The three men left the restaurant together, walking past four tables where agents sat. Burt took side streets back to the FBI office. When he pulled into the parking lot, Pirog, O'Sullivan and four other agents were waiting for him.

They took Burt upstairs, dismantled the transmitter and debriefed him. "It sounds great," Pirog said. "This should do it."

"It better," Burt said.

Pirog called Jonathan Goldstein, spoke for a while, then handed the phone to Burt.

"I think we're in good shape," Jonathan said. "I'd like you to come in at eight-thirty tomorrow morning. I also want to send two agents to your home at about seven-thirty so they can be with Laurie for the day. Okay?"

"That's fine," Burt said. "But am I going before a grand jury tomorrow or not?"

"Just do me a favor," Jonathan said. "Be here at eight-thirty."

Burt left Pirog's office exhausted, but high with anticipation. This had to be post time. It just would have been nice, he thought, if he could have put a few more pieces in the puzzle. Serota—Andy—Investors Funding. How did they fit in?

The speculation ended as he drove into Fort Lee and his Chevy sputtered to a halt. When the engine wouldn't turn over, Burt walked to a phone booth, called a garage for a tow truck and got a ride to a cottage party that was now almost over.

"Where have you been?" his candidates asked as he walked in the door.

"Out campaigning for you," Burt said.

13

Friday, May 31.

Burt had been up several times during the night, rolling over to check the time and staring out the window at the Manhattan skyline. When the doorbell rang at seven-thirty, he was already dressed in the blue and white suit Laurie had laid out the night before. He was on his second cigar. A young couple in their twenties was standing outside his door. Burt recognized the tall blonde woman in the gray pantsuit from the night before. She had been sitting in an adjacent booth at the Red Coach.

"Nice to see you," Burt greeted her. "I was going to send some wine over to your table, but I figured you don't drink on the job."

The agent, whose name was Pat, laughed and introduced Burt to her partner, Craig, whose baby-faced, clean-cut look would have seemed more appropriate on a college campus in the fifties.

As the three walked to the living room, Laurie emerged in a bathrobe, offered a sleepy hello and went to the kitchen to make coffee. Pat and Craig looked over the two phones and decided to hook up their taping equipment to the one in the bedroom. Sutton and Diaco had been "sat on" all night, Pat explained, and she was under instructions to monitor all incoming calls.

This was joyous news to Burt. If Sutton and Diaco were under surveillance, it meant that something was about to happen. Today—thirteen days after Diaco's first contact, five days after the money was passed and four days before the election—today had to be it.

It was almost eight when Burt kissed Laurie good-bye and headed for the elevator. There was a moment of panic when he got to his parking space. The Chevy wasn't there. Then he remembered that it had conked out and was in a garage, that he had made arrangements to use his mother's Riviera.

"Christ," he thought, "I really must be nervous."

Instead of parking in the lot across the street, Burt followed Jonathan's instructions and pulled into the underground garage of the Federal Building. His feeling that this small item—parking in Bruce or Jonathan's spot—foretold the big drama that lay ahead, evaporated with the gas fumes as he turned the engine off.

"Where you going?" a husky black attendant asked him.

"Jonathan Goldstein told me to park in his space or in Bruce Goldstein's," Burt said.

"Their spaces is filled," the attendant said.

"Well, what should I do?" Burt asked.

"That's your problem," the attendant said.

Burt called upstairs, got Bruce on the phone and explained the problem. Bruce asked to speak to the attendant, but the black man refused to yield an inch to the Executive Assistant U.S. Attorney. "The rules is the rules," he said.

Dick Shapiro arrived a few minutes later and convinced the attendant to let Burt use the space reserved for Congressman Peter Rodino. Then he took Burt up in the elevator and led him quickly past the law library and inner sanctum of cubicles before depositing him in a conference room.

Bruce walked in a few minutes later and greeted Burt

warmly. "Well, this is it," he said. "You'll be going before a grand jury soon, but I don't know exactly when. We'll come get you when it's time."

Soon after Burt had left for Newark, Laurie had changed into jeans and a T-shirt, straightened up the bedroom and set about making Pat and Craig comfortable. At nine, Pat called the FBI office. "Sutton was just served," she said when she got off. "They got him just after the chauffeur drove the kids to school in his Rolls Royce. They're supposed to be laying it on Diaco right about now. I think the subpoenas are for an appearance before the grand jury at ten-thirty."

Twenty minutes later the phone rang and Craig went to the bedroom to turn on the recorder.

"Hello, is Burt in?" Diaco asked.

"No, he isn't," Laurie said. "Who's calling, please?"

"Okay, I'll get him later," Diaco said.

"Can I take a message?" Laurie asked.

"No, that's all right," Diaco said before hanging up. "I'll get him."

"I didn't like the sound of that," Laurie said to the two agents.

"Neither did I," Craig said. "Does he know where you live?"

"He's been here once," Laurie said. "But you told me they're under surveillance."

"*Were* under surveillance," Pat corrected her. "They dropped it after the subpoenas were served. I don't know why they decided to do that. What the hell are we supposed to do if he shows up?"

Pat called her office again for instructions. She listened intently, then got off and clapped her hands. "Okay, here's what we're going to do," she said. "If he comes, Craig and I will hide in the bedroom and see what happens."

This was Laurie's first contact with the FBI. Her stomach began to churn.

"I don't want to get too personal," she said, "but do the two of you happen to have guns?"

Craig nodded.

"I'm glad to hear that," Laurie said, "because to tell you the truth, I'm not exactly thrilled about being used as some kind of bait."

Shortly after ten, the intercom buzzed and the doorman announced that a package was on the way up. Laurie looked at Pat. "I'm sure this whole scene has made me a little paranoid," she said, "but I'm not expecting any packages."

The doorbell rang. Pat and Craig moved out of sight and Laurie took a small box wrapped in brown paper from a delivery man. She carried it to the two agents and put it down.

"Well?" she asked.

"Well, what?" Craig volunteered.

"Well, who's going to open it?" Laurie demanded.

Pat picked up the package, looked at it and passed it to Craig. He looked it over, shook it gingerly and handed it back. Pat shook it some more, then handed it to Laurie.

"What is this, Abbott and Costello?" Laurie asked. She took off the wrappings and opened the box. Inside was a porcelain plate and a card.

"Jesus," Laurie said after reading the note, "it's a gift from some friends. Sunday is our first anniversary. This just shows you where my head is at."

Craig offered his best wishes and Laurie abandoned her fantasy, born less than an hour before, of trading in her leathercrafts and woodworking for an FBI shield.

By noon Burt was climbing the walls. He had been alone for three hours now, and the room was heavy with cigar smoke. He had tried doing his first crossword puzzle. He was pacing.

"Let's go," Bruce said as he opened the door. "We're on."

Burt followed Bruce and Dick to the elevator. He started when he saw Dick press the "Up" button.

"Hey," he said. "What's going on? I thought we were going to the courthouse."

"We are," Bruce said, "but we want to go over a few things

147

with you first and it's quieter on the sixth floor."

The sixth floor was the repository for all the paperwork knocked out below, and was uninhabited except for two guards. Dick and Bruce escorted Burt to a bare room and brought in some chairs.

"We'll be going over in a few minutes," Bruce said, "but first we want to ask you some questions. Do you know a man by the name of Arthur Sutton?"

"Are you putting me on?" Burt asked.

"C'mon, Burt," Dick said with annoyance. "We're going over some questions with you. Get it?"

Burt got it. He was embarrassed at not having picked up on it immediately. He felt worse for having thought that they were questioning his story. Why, he asked himself, was there this lingering sense of guilt?

"I'm sorry," he told Dick. "I didn't get you at first. The answer to your question is yes."

The questions unrolled and with them the case. Everything was cut and dried. Each could be answered with a yes or a no. Bruce did the interrogating, and sometimes he would stumble and go back to improve the wording.

By twelve-thirty they had finished. Bruce looked at his watch, nodded to Dick and said they could go now. They took the elevator to the lobby and walked across the street to the court-house. Bruce and Dick walked on either side. Burt reached into his pocket and put on sunglasses.

If the U.S. Attorney's Office seemed like the antiseptic oper-ating room of a skilled surgeon, the Federal Courthouse looked like the back room of an old abortionist. Dick and Bruce led Burt through a maze of dingy corridors, past figures huddling together in whispered conversations. Each time they ap-proached an intersection, Dick would get to it first, look both ways, then motion for the others to continue. It was evident to Burt what this precaution was for. Diaco and Sutton had been before the grand jury first, and the prosecutors wanted to avoid a chance meeting.

So did Burt. The thought of running into Diaco awakened physical fear. Sutton would be different. If they were to see each other, Burt imagined, he would feel sadness and guilt. He had never thought of Diaco as someone's husband or father, but he had met Sutton's wife and had liked her.

They did not meet. Bruce and Dick finally stopped in front of a door and began speaking with a man in his late forties who was wearing a seedy suit, white patent leather shoes and dark glasses. This guy made Diaco look like a church elder. His name was Sal. He was a U.S. Marshal. With Sal posted outside as guard, Dick and Bruce led Burt through the door to a small anteroom. Bruce said he and Dick would go before the grand jury alone first and would be back to get him shortly. When they had opened the inner door and disappeared, Burt sat down on a wooden bench, put his chin in his hands and tried to relax himself with deep breathing.

A few minutes later the door opened and Bruce stuck his head inside. "You can come in now," he said.

He led Burt past two rows of jurors and asked him to be seated on a raised witness stand. The jury foreman sat next to him. There was no judge. As his eyes began to focus in this large, cheerless room, Burt looked around. The jurors, perhaps twenty in all, were middle-aged. All wore somber clothes and expressions to match. Nearly half were women; only one was black. The windows were closed and the room was heavy with dead air.

As the clerk swore him in, Burt wished he had worn a more conservative suit. The only person close to him in age was the stenographer, who sat expressionless, his fingers moving effortlessly.

"Would you tell the ladies and gentlemen of the grand jury your name, sir?" Bruce began.

Burt leaned forward to the microphone and cleared his throat. "My name is Burt Ross," he said.

"Where do you reside, Mr. Ross?"

"I reside in Fort Lee, New Jersey."

As Bruce set the scene, Burt tried to make eye contact with some jurors. He smiled at a gray-haired woman. She looked through him. He nodded at the black man. No response. "My God," he thought, "do these people know I'm the good guy? They look like they're getting ready to indict me."

Bruce droned on. "Mayor Ross, did there come a time, sir, in substance, when Mr. Sutton and Mr. Diaco offered you the sum of five-hundred-thousand dollars to persuade you to use your influence in causing the board of adjustment of the Borough of Fort Lee to adjourn a meeting that was then scheduled for May 22, 1974, at which meeting variance applications relating to the development of the George Washington Plaza were to be considered?"

Burt stopped looking at the jurors and concentrated on Bruce. He tried to sound convincing. He was sweating.

"Mayor Ross, I have no further questions," Bruce said twenty minutes later. Burt did not immediately respond. "You may step down, sir," Bruce said. Burt tripped getting off the stand.

The clerk led him back to the anteroom and told him to wait. Bruce and Dick remained inside. A few minutes passed and the stenographer entered and walked toward the door leading to the hall. Burt looked to him for a sign but got none. Then the man stopped, turned to face Burt and said softly, "I just want you to know that you've restored my faith in government."

Bruce and Dick came in ten minutes later. "Congratulations," Bruce said. "You were an excellent witness."

"Will there be indictments today?" Burt asked.

"Everything is progressing well," Dick said. "We want you to stay with the marshals for a little while, and then we'll come get you."

150

Dick stuck his head into the hallway and nodded to someone. The marshal who came in was not Sal, but Jim, a tall, athletic looking blond about Burt's age. He escorted the mayor down the hall, walking slightly in front of him, to a small room which was sparsely furnished with old desks and chairs.

"Make yourself comfortable," Jim said to Burt. Then he turned his attention to the only other person in the room, a small, dark-complected man who looked like he came from Sal's neighborhood. For the next hour and a half the two marshals talked about making out vouchers and Jim's recent trip to Florida. Burt sat and waited.

By two-thirty Laurie and the FBI agents had gotten tired of playing Scrabble. The phone had rung several times and Craig had jumped up to activate the recorder, but on each occasion it had been someone calling to ask about campaign material or to say they had heard Carl Stokes was back in town. "Don't worry," Laurie told them all. "Everything is being taken care of. Just trust me."

The phone rang again at three. This time it was a reporter who had been moonlighting as a publicist for Serota's slate.

"Laurie," he began, "I never owed anyone an apology more than I owe you people."

"Excuse me?" Laurie said.

"Haven't you heard?" the reporter blurted. "I just got back from a press conference that Jonathan Goldstein held. Sutton and Diaco were indicted. Burt is a hero. Is he there?"

"No," Laurie said, "but I'll tell him you called. Thanks."

Laurie got off the phone and raised a fist. "It must have gone really well," she said to Pat and Craig. "Burt must be on Cloud Nine."

Actually, he was still in the marshals' office, unaware that a major press conference had just ended across the street. Jonathan Goldstein had called him "a courageous public official who was offered more money than most men make in a lifetime, who deserves our praise for his courageous act and his determination." The U.S. Attorney said that Burt had cooperated at "great personal risk" and that "this office will take all necessary steps to protect Mayor Ross's security." Flattering words, but Burt had heard none of them. What he had heard was the two marshals' continuing small talk, and as he listened to Jim wax euphoric about Disney World, he grew restless. Shortly after three, he asked if he could make a phone call.

"God, it sure is boring here," he greeted Laurie. "What's with you?"

Laurie thought Burt was putting her on and let him continue. When she realized he was serious, she shouted out the news.

Burt's reaction wasn't exactly what Laurie had expected. "Shit," he said.

"Are you crazy?" she asked.

He assured her that he wasn't. Yes, there was a moment or two of relief that it was now out. But then came tremendous anger that as the curtain went up for the final act, the star of the show was being kept offstage. Burt's mood changed only when Laurie reminded him of the political impact of the event. "I only wish I could see Serota's face," he said.

By the time they hung up, Burt couldn't wait to get back to Fort Lee, to campaign in front of supermarkets, to attend the last round of cottage parties, to witness the returns of election night. His reverie was interrupted when Sal walked in and said they could go over to Jonathan's office. He and Jim took Burt across the street, looking in all directions and making sure the mayor was wedged between them. The close attention struck Burt as both comic and exciting. That there was something he was being protected from never registered.

Jonathan and his assistants were in shirt-sleeves when Burt arrived. For the first time since he had known them, they seemed relaxed. The U.S. Attorney briefed the mayor on what had taken place, but added little to what Burt already knew. Then, in what sounded like a casual afterthought, he said, "For the time being, I think it advisable to provide you and Laurie with protection."

The subject still left Burt unmoved. If this was the U.S. Attorney's way of dramatizing the event, it was fine with him. It would also dramatize the end of the campaign. The idea of appearing in public with a bodyguard at his side was rather appealing.

"Okay," he told Jonathan, "I respect your judgment. So how about telling whoever is going to protect me to take me home? I've got a lot of things to do tonight."

Jonathan's voice changed. It became hushed and official. "Burt," he said, "we think it is extremely important that you leave town for a few days."

"Why?" Burt asked uneasily.

"I don't want to go into details," Jonathan said. "If you respect my judgment, then I ask you to accept that it would be unsafe and imprudent for you to be in Fort Lee right now."

Burt had spent too much time putting this whole cake together to be told now that he couldn't be around to lick the icing. "I do respect your judgment," he said, "but I'm not a child. I don't like to be told to do something without being given a reason. Is there really some danger or what?"

Jonathan tapped on the desk with his fingers. "Look," he said, "I've already told you about Diaco's phone call to Laurie. That's the first thing we're not happy about. But it's more than just that. What you have done is going to affect a lot of people. Some of them are very bad people. I shouldn't have to convince you that right now, when feelings are running high, you shouldn't be walking around in public."

Burt sighed. "Okay," he told Jonathan, "I'll stay out of town on two conditions. The first is that we get back in time to vote on Tuesday. The second is that you don't hole us up in one of those highway motels I've read about."

"Where would you like to go?" Jonathan asked.

"How about Atlanta?" Burt asked. "We have good friends there, and there shouldn't be any trouble getting marshals."

Telephone calls began. People conferred in the hall. An hour later it was set. They would leave Newark on an eight-thirty flight. Sal and another marshal would fly down with Burt and Laurie and hand them over to the marshals in Atlanta.

As Burt prepared to leave Jonathan's office, Sutton and Diaco were being arraigned in the courthouse across the street. Both were released on $100,000 personal recognizance bonds, with bail to be posted the following Monday. Each had his travel restricted to New York and New Jersey. Their passports were seized. Diaco was instructed to turn over his pistol to federal authorities.

Sal, his partner Luke and Jim took Burt down to his car. They formed a protective shield around him, checking out the staircase as they rounded each turn. When they got to the garage, they looked under the hood of the Riviera, opened the trunk and reached into the tailpipes. Jim walked over to the marshals' car, pulled a gun from the trunk and laid it on the back seat of Burt's car.

"What the hell is that, a submachine gun?" Burt asked.

"Why don't you drive, and we'll call it a good rifle," Luke said.

As Sal got in the front seat and adjusted his holster, Burt no longer thought of this as a joke. He held his breath as he started the ignition. He started looking around as soon as they hit the street.

"I'm sweating," he said as they left Newark. "Mind if I roll down the window?"

"Keep the window up," Sal told him. "You can turn on the air conditioning if you're hot."

"Is all this protection really necessary?" Burt asked.

"Just do what we tell you to and you'll be safe," Luke said.

It was past six when they pulled up to Burt's building. The doorman rushed to greet him, then froze. Sal had pulled the gun out of the back seat and was handing it to Jim. "Wait here for us," he told Jim.

While Burt took a shower and Laurie packed, his father manned the phones. They hadn't stopped ringing for two hours, he said. Reporters were trying to get through. Friends wanted to know if Burt was all right. Laurie's mother had just called for the second time.

While Burt grabbed his first bite of the day, Laurie headed for the door with the garbage. She got her first pangs when Sal insisted on accompanying her. "Don't worry about it," Burt said when she returned. "He just wanted to make sure you didn't fall into the incinerator."

Someone had turned on the television, and all conversation stopped when Fort Lee was mentioned. After showing a filmed report of Jonathan's press conference, Jim Hartz turned to Carl Stokes.

"Carl," he said, "you've taken a special interest in this Fort Lee story. Can you give us an idea of some of the events that led up to the indictments today?"

"Yeah," Burt laughed. "Explain it to us, Carl."

"Well, Jim," Stokes said, "twelve months ago Gordon Thomas and I went into Fort Lee and we were just convinced that no man was going to put seventeen million dollars into property and gamble on the variances being granted. As a consequence, we followed up on it. I think WNBC was the only media that kept the spotlight on it, kept the heat on it, and I think can take credit today for having led to today's events."

"Are you kidding?" Laurie screamed at the set.

"The guy is out of this world," Burt muttered.

A few hurried good-byes and they were off, Sal and Luke running interference. "Don't get alarmed," Burt whispered to Laurie in the elevator, "but there's a submachine gun in the car. I think these guys have been watching too many movies."

As they sped past the film crews and reporters who were

huddling in the light rain that had started to fall, Burt tried to keep his wife's spirits up. "Maybe they think we just got married and want to throw rice," he said.

The humor didn't last long. On the way to the airport, Sal turned to Laurie.

"Do you have any kids?" he asked.

"No," Laurie said.

"That's good," Sal suggested. "This is no time to have kids."

On board the plane, Sal went up to speak to the captain and Burt and Laurie settled back to their Bloody Marys.

"It's been a hell of a first year," Burt toasted his wife.

"I hope we're around for the second anniversary," Laurie answered.

As their plane flew over New Jersey, quite another scene was unfolding back in Fort Lee. Burt's candidates had just arrived at a cottage party that was being thrown in their honor in an elegant apartment. Nathan Serota had asked to be invited, and the hostess had reluctantly agreed. The talk all centered on Burt and the story that had gotten such heavy play on the evening news shows. Serota listened quietly to the adulation for a few minutes, then interrupted with a commentary of his own.

Serota told them not to be fooled by all this garbage. He knew Burt Ross and he knew the developing business. He was a developer himself. This whole thing just didn't add up. Sutton wouldn't have bought that land without a commitment. He thought that the mayor had some kind of a deal going, but got cold feet. There are no heroes in politics Serota concluded.

When Burt and Laurie arrived in Atlanta, Sal and Luke handed them over to a marshal who drove them to a motel on the outskirts of the city. At the reservations desk, they found that a room was waiting for a Mr. and Mrs. Bart Moss. "Now that is what I call amateurish," Laurie said.

While Burt and Laurie read about themselves on the front pages of the New York papers Saturday morning, the citizens of Fort Lee were also reading about their mayor. They saw one paper, however, that wasn't for sale in Atlanta. Roy Sampath had gone to press with his pre-election issue of *The Independent* before the indictments broke. And although he had frantically tried to retrieve the copies that had been distributed, it was too late.

"The hopes of developer Arthur Sutton to build a $250 million hi-rise commercial office and shopping center at Bridge Plaza will hinge on the outcome of Tuesday's election," Sampath had written. "It is widely expected that the . . . megastructure will be erected if the incumbents are re-elected . . . We can only hope that the Fort Lee voter would . . . send Ross back to New York City by defeating his front men at the polls. The issue in this primary election is Ross. Boss Ross. Fort Lee voters have never had a clearer choice."

Burt called the U.S. Attorney on Monday afternoon. "We're having a wonderful time and I thank the government for its hospitality," he said. "Now, how do we arrange for me to get back in time to vote tomorrow?"

"Let me be very candid with you," Jonathan replied. "I do not want you in Fort Lee now under any circumstances. It is the last place in the world you should be."

"But you told me I could vote," Burt groaned.

"Your vote won't make any difference," Jonathan said.

"That's not the point," Burt pleaded. "I want to go back. I mean, is there a threat or isn't there?"

"There may be a threat," Jonathan said, "and it isn't just Diaco we're talking about. You'd be a sitting duck in Fort Lee for some nut who didn't like heroes or for some small-time thug who wants to impress the big shots by knocking off the guy that blew the whistle. I can't tell you it will happen. They don't tell us these things in advance."

It was another one of those "how can you argue if it's the right thing to do?" situations.

"How long do you want us out of town?" Burt asked.

"The trial should begin in early fall," Jonathan said. "Why

don't we play it safe until then. It's the summer. The birds are singing. Why don't you and Laurie go someplace and listen to them."

"Okay," Burt said after talking with Laurie, "but only if we go to Martha's Vineyard. We've already paid for a summer house there, and it doesn't matter if there are no marshals around. The place is set back off a dirt road. Bloodhounds couldn't find us."

Jonathan agreed. He told Burt to keep a low profile during the summer and to use a false name. He said that he'd want the mayor to come back to Newark several times to begin preparing for the trial.

Burt and Laurie flew to New York the next afternoon, which was primary day. As their plane circled LaGuardia, Burt looked down at the George Washington Bridge and the clusters of apartment buildings stretching up from Fort Lee. "Vote column one, you mothers," he exhorted as a stewardess stood by scratching her head.

Burt and Laurie's parents met them at the airport with more clothes and birth control pills. It was a less than happy reunion. As they watched their son being shepherded around by marshals, Dave and Rose Ross kept asking how long this would continue. "I've been a cop all my life," Bill Miller said. "I knew it would end up like this."

As the marshals led Burt and Laurie to their connecting flight, Burt looked back over his shoulder. "What's a nice Jewish boy like me doing in a situation like this?" he shouted.

The polls were just closing in Fort Lee when Burt and Laurie arrived at their house on the Vineyard. Nearly three hundred of Burt's Democrats had gathered at the recreation center to await the returns. The mayor's parents and in-laws were there. George Karageorge, who owned the local diner, was setting food on the table. Pete McGuire, who had once called Burt a young whippersnapper, was pouring the drinks. Everyone had one eye on the door, hoping that Burt would make a surprise entrance.

The phone in the recreation center rang shortly after nine. Burt had left his secluded house to drive three miles to the nearest pay phone. The first words he heard were "Mazel Tov." He had done it. Four thousand people had voted, twice the normal figure for an off-year election. Twenty-five hundred of them had voted for Mosolino, Weinkrantz and Lauricella. Burt's candidates had sixty-three percent of the vote. It was a landslide.

The losing slate came without their leader, offered their congratulations and quickly left. Mamma Gallo lifted her glass of wine and offered a toast. "God bless our mayor," she said.

Burt drove back to the house after the phone call, kissed Laurie and made a fire. Nathan Serota could not have slept as well. That his candidates had lost was only part of the nightmare. The biggest part was yet to come: For Serota, for others, the election was over. Now, something even more important was at stake.

The only ripple to Burt's and Laurie's summer of happiness came toward the end of July. Dave Flanders was the local real estate broker and one of the few people to whom Burt had disclosed his real identity. One afternoon Flanders stopped by to tell Burt about an upsetting incident: Four "hoody-looking" men had just come into his office and said they wanted to rent a house on the beach. But as he drove them around, all they wanted to know was whether he had rented any houses recently to a young couple from New Jersey. Their own car had Jersey plates. And when Flanders leaned in to say good-bye, he had seen a pistol on the back seat.

Burt chose not to tell the U.S. Attorney about what had happened. He was having too good a time to risk being transferred to a guarded motel. Instead, he grew a beard, shied away from public places and double-checked to make sure his door was locked each night.

In the outside world, public reaction to the case continued to grow. "All politicians shouldn't be tarnished by the misdeeds of a few power-hungry men who flaunted the law while they basked in the sunshine of Key Biscayne and San Clemente," columnist Jack Anderson wrote. "The stories should be written, too, of the honorable politicians—men like the courageous small-town Mayor who turned down a $500,000 bribe and risked the wrath of the Mafia rather than compromise his integrity. His name, Burt Ross, deserves a big headline."

Hundreds of letters from around the country poured into Borough Hall, where Councilman Max Lazarus was filling in admirably for Burt. "I'm praying that no harm will come to you and your family," a Tennessee man wrote. "Many people will remember your name if you ever decide to run for national office. Good luck and thank you. P.S. The bass fishing here is great. If you ever come to Tennessee, it would be an honor for me to meet you."

Closer to home, the reactions were more mixed. Some thought Burt should have refused the offer and kept his mouth shut. Others continued to believe that he had been in on the deal and gotten cold feet at the last minute. A local newspaper editor expressed even darker concerns. Were the rumors true, he wanted to know in an off-the-record interview, that Burt had once been confined to a mental institution? That his marriage was a convenient screen to cover up his homosexuality? That the U.S. Attorney had been the best man at his wedding?

Sutton and Diaco did nothing to diminish public speculation. They couldn't wait to get to trial, they told the press, because the evidence would prove that they had never initiated a bribe. They had been the victims of extortion.

When word of all this got back to Burt, he grew restless. A trial date had been set for October 7. In the meantime, he had no way to defend himself from Martha's Vineyard. "If Sutton and Diaco are acquitted," he said to Laurie, "people are going to conclude that I'm guilty."

Back in Newark, the U.S. Attorney had spent June and July analyzing the tapes. But the more he went over what he had, the more he understood how much more there was to get. Burt's probing during the taped conversations had raised many questions. What Jonathan Goldstein needed now was some way to provide the answers. He worked late into summer nights with Bruce Goldstein and Dick Shapiro. He tried unsuccessfully to subpoena Sutton's business records. He began looking into Investors Funding. He kept hoping for a break.

By late August, Burt's concern about the trial had turned to alarm. "What the hell is going on?" he asked Jonathan during a phone call. "Why don't you want me in Newark to start getting prepared? I'm sure the other side isn't taking the summer off."

Jonathan told Burt to keep cool. "I also have other cases to worry about," he said.

"Well, I don't know," Burt said disconsolately. "It just doesn't seem like any way to get your star witness ready."

The U.S. Attorney told the mayor to relax. What he neglected to mention was that he had a very different reason for taking his time now: Burt was no longer his star witness.

14

On September 10, Burt and Laurie were listening to a news broadcast when they heard an item that caused the mayor to leap from the dinner table and throw his salad in the air with both glee and disbelief.

A federal grand jury in Newark had just handed down three-count indictments against Norman Dansker, Stephen Haymes, Donald Orenstein and Warner Norton, the top officers of Investors Funding Corporation, and against Andrew Valentine and Joseph Diaco, the heads of Valentine Electric Company. They were charged with the attempted bribe of the mayor of Fort Lee and the actual bribe of another borough official, a member of the local Parking Authority. He was also indicted. His name was Nathan Serota.

The involvement of Investors Funding made Burt feel like a giant-killer. It also stunned him. "My God," he said to Laurie, "I had my suspicions, but this is unbelievable. I just wish I had known what the hell I started."

Serota was something else. Burt had never really believed Diaco's hints that the multimillionaire had been paid off, but here it was—the indictment of Burt's worst enemy, the man who had headed the opposition to the project which it now seemed he had been bribed to support, the guy who had been telling everyone that the mayor must have been in on the deal and gotten cold feet. There were barely words to describe Burt's feeling. It was sweet vindication. It was poetic justice.

When he heard that the trial had been reset for the early part of 1975, Burt called Jonathan Goldstein to announce that he was returning to Fort Lee. The U.S. Attorney told him to stay away. "I'm coming back," Burt said. "I'll stop in to see you on the way home."

On September 15, Burt and Laurie loaded their valises and the pup they had acquired into the car and took the ferry to the mainland. As they drove south through Providence and New Haven, Laurie verged on tears. Everything seemed so ugly. What would happen to the intimacy she had developed with her husband? Burt was high with anticipation. He was tired of experiencing second hand all the excitement the case had generated. Now he could get back to the action. He could enjoy the fruits of his labor.

"Don't worry, Poops," he assured his wife as they waited out a traffic jam in the East Bronx. "Nothing between us has to change. We can still have our privacy."

They drove to Newark in the morning. It took half an hour for Jonathan to come get them. When he did, he asked Laurie to remain outside his office. There were some things he wanted to go over with Burt alone, he said. Laurie sent an angry glance at her husband. He pretended not to notice it.

There was a simple point Jonathan wanted to make to Burt. To help him get it across, he had assembled Bruce Goldstein, Dick Shapiro and two other assistants who had worked on the case. The point was this: They didn't want Burt and Laurie to go back to Fort Lee until after the trial."

"I'm going back today," Burt said.

"The trial is just a few months away," Jonathan urged. "We can relocate you somewhere for that time. Why take any chances?"

"Bullshit," Burt said. "I've listened to you people since this

163

whole thing began. Now I'm going to do it my way. I'm the mayor and I'm going to do my job. I don't need another vacation."

Jonathan warned Burt that he would be a very visible target in Fort Lee, but this time Burt wasn't buying. "I'll always be a target in public life," he said. "I might as well start getting used to it."

"Everything will quiet down after the trial," Bruce said.

"I may be crazy," Burt replied, "but I have a feeling that your main concern about me is that I'll talk to the press and say something to jeopardize the case."

Dick Shapiro's face reddened. "Listen, buddy," he said, shaking his finger in Burt's face, "if that's what bothered us, we'd say so. We don't have to play games with you."

"To tell you the truth," Burt shot back, "I don't care anymore what's on your mind. Unless you can get a court order to keep me away, I'm going home."

When Jonathan realized that Burt wasn't budging, he threw his next card on the table. "If you absolutely insist on going back," he said, "it's got to be with twenty-four-hour protection. That includes your apartment. It may not be too comfortable."

"You can move a division in with me," Burt said. "As long as I go back."

Jonathan reached for the phone, called the head of the local U.S. Marshals' Office and told him to come over with Police Chief Dalton. "We have a lot of coordinating to do," he said.

Laurie was still upset when Burt came out to wait with her while arrangements were made. Her mood worsened when the marshal and police chief joined them. The two officers offered a graphic description of the blanket security they were going to provide, and an even more vivid picture of the dangers the security was intended to avert. They talked about firebombings, kidnappings, snipers and dismembered bodies."

"Burt, let's go back to the Vineyard," Laurie pleaded.

"Just give it a try," Burt answered. "We can always change our minds."

A small caravan of marshals accompanied Burt and Laurie to Fort Lee. Two dozen cops volunteered to work as guards in their off hours. A marshal who introduced himself as Che Guevera passed out a ten-page directive on procedures. Jonathan had decided that the Fort Lee police would do the day-to-day work. The marshals would be available for crowd scenes.

When they arrived at Burt and Laurie's apartment, the marshals walked in first, guns drawn. They checked to make sure no one was inside. They pulled down the shades and told Burt and Laurie never to walk near a window.

Within hours they had installed burglar alarms, applied tape to the windows, changed the lock on the door and put "panic buttons" in the living room, bedroom and kitchen. If anything came up, they explained, Burt or Laurie could press the button, which would set off an alarm in police headquarters and bring out the troops.

Then they described the changes in lifestyle that would have to be made. The cops would always answer the phone first. They would check all incoming mail for bombs. Burt and Laurie would have to change their regular shopping habits, never going to the same cleaner or supermarket twice in a row. And anywhere they went, armed guards would always be with them.

Laurie left the suitcases unopened. "I'm sorry," she told Burt, "but I'm not sure how much of this I can take. If it's your decision, you may have to live with it alone until after the trial."

Burt returned to work the next morning. Two plainclothesmen drove him to L.F. Rothschild in an unmarked car and kept in radio communication with headquarters under the code name "Foxtrot One." Each of them wore a colored armband. "If we come under attack," one of them explained, "they're a signal to the New York City cops which side we're on."

Later that afternoon the cops drove Burt back to Fort Lee.

The mayor had decided to keep his full beard and shoulder-length hair. As he walked into Borough Hall wearing a floppy white hat and sunglasses, a corncob pipe jutting from his mouth, no one looked up.

"May I help you?" said his secretary, glancing up from her desk.

"Helen, it's me," Burt said.

"My God," Helen Cole said.

Handshakes and hugs followed as the word spread and other Borough employees clustered around. By day's end Chief Dalton had given them all identification cards and sealed off Borough Hall from the curious townspeople who had gathered to catch a glimpse of their mayor.

Burt enjoyed the reunions. Surrounded by armed guards, he cut the ribbon at the new police station. The governor came to town to congratulate him. The volunteer firemen awarded him a pair of brass balls. Laurie, who had become "Foxtrot Two," remained cooped up in the apartment, working halfheartedly on the coffee table she had started to build that spring.

The regular monthly meeting of the mayor and council fell shortly after Burt and Laurie returned. There was no announcement that Burt would attend, but since the papers had carried stories that he was back, the marshals and cops expected a crowd. All entrances to Borough Hall were guarded. Three marshals frisked all visitors after guiding them through a metal scanning device. Two cops with rifles were stationed on the roof. Marshals stood behind the mayor's seat. Plainclothesmen lined the walls of the fifty-year-old chamber.

Just before the meeting, Burt and Laurie were getting dressed in their bedroom when there was a knock on the door. Burt opened it to find a marshal holding a bulletproof vest.

"What the hell is that for?" he asked.

"Please put it on," the marshal said. "We understand that there will be a lot of people there tonight."

Burt put the vest under his blue and white striped jacket and made nervous jokes about how everyone would think he had gained weight. Laurie donned a dress for the first time in four months.

They were driven separately to Borough Hall in unmarked police cars. The oxygen units and first aid kits in the cars, they were told, were just a precaution. When they arrived, they were taken through the basement up a flight of stairs and kept aside in a small anteroom. When Burt's fellow councilmen realized he was there, they tried to approach him. The marshals kept them away.

In the council chamber, four hundred people had gathered, filling the wooden benches and overflowing into the hall. The marshals turned another hundred away at the door. The councilmen entered first and took their seats on either side of the borough attorney and clerk, who had also been equipped with a bulletproof vest. Then everyone waited, eyes focused on the side door. It opened at eight-thirty. Three plainclothesmen came out first, hands riveted to their holsters. Laurie followed and was escorted quickly to a front-row seat. Then two marshals came out. Burt was just behind them.

As the mayor mounted the platform and walked to his seat, there was a second or two of silence as it registered on the audience that it was Burt. Then came the roar. For five minutes, everyone but Councilwoman Pearl Moskowitz stood and applauded. Burt motioned for silence, and when it still didn't stop, he sat there motionless, looking out at all the familiar faces.

The meeting was brief. Many, including a few of Burt's enemies, rose to say how proud they were to know him. No one seemed anxious to debate an amendment to the rent-leveling ordinance or to discuss the merits of widening a road. When it was over, everyone was kept in the room until Burt and Laurie had left the building.

For the next few weeks the twenty-four hour protection and the tension between Burt and Laurie continued.

"I'm sorry, Burt," Laurie said one night, "but I just can't

handle this kind of life. Either you do something about it or I will."

Burt did something. In the middle of October he met with Chief Dalton and the marshals. "You may be worried about losing a mayor," he told them, "but I'm concerned about losing a wife. You've got to make life more tolerable for her."

Dalton responded. He instructed the cops who were guarding Laurie to consult her more and let her out of the house. He permitted her to go to a dude ranch with her father for a few days. He gave Burt and Laurie leave to spend a weekend on Martha's Vineyard.

As the weeks passed without incident, the whole protection routine became a lively topic of conversation. It also caused Burt and Laurie to get some ribbing. One night, they were having dinner at some friends' house when one of their burly guards sauntered out of the kitchen. "I don't mean to interrupt your dinner, mayor," he said, "but didn't you forget something?"

"What's that?" Burt asked.

"To call you mother," the cop said.

Several people wanted to know how Burt and Laurie could have any love life with all the cops around. "It's simple," Laurie explained. "I've worked out a code with the guards. When Burt and I are in the mood, I just tell them that Foxtrot One and Foxtrot Two are going to tango."

The one scare came in early November, a few days after Burt's three council candidates had swept the general election following a virtually uncontested campaign. A woman who lived next to Burt and Laurie, and who had an adjoining terrace, knocked frantically on their door one night. "I just got this horrible phone call," she told the cop who let her in. "Some man with a deep voice called my unlisted number and said there was someone who lived next to me that he didn't like, and that he was going to ask for my help in the near future. He said I better cooperate or there would be trouble."

An extra guard was put on, but nothing materialized. For Burt and Laurie the threat was an anxious reminder that there was in fact a reason for all the protection. At least that's what they thought.

From the time of Burt's return, Jonathan Goldstein had assured him that he was doing all he could to get federal funds to pay for the off-duty cops Fort Lee was providing as protection. Burt never thought it would be a problem. He was wrong.

The bill for the protection was running nearly two thousand dollars a week, and by November it had begun to cut into the borough's treasury. Burt pushed Jonathan for action. If the money didn't come soon, he said, the council would have to appropriate publicly a special fund. There was no reason why he should be put through that embarrassment.

Jonathan asked Burt to wait a few more days. He would personally speak with Henry Petersen, who headed the Criminal Justice Division, and with U.S. Attorney General William Saxbe.

The U.S. Attorney got back to Burt the next week. "I'm afraid I have bad news," he said. "The Justice Department has decided that you don't need protection. They say that they won't put up the money, but if you want, they'll relocate you and give you a new identity."

Burt was momentarily speechless. "I just want to make sure I'm hearing you right," he finally said. "Are you telling me that the U.S. Attorney who is handling the case doesn't have the power to decide whether his witness needs protection?"

Jonathan's voice was filled with humiliation and rage. For the first time, Burt heard him shout. "Those damn people," he said. "They only know how to protect crooks."

Burt ended the conversation quickly. He called Chief Dalton and told him to withdraw all the protection and to remove the equipment. "The borough is not going to pay for this," he said. "This is a federal case."

Dalton's response was out of gentle character. "Those fucking bastards," he shouted. "They spend hundreds of thousands of dollars to protect people like Nixon and Agnew, but people like you they throw to the wolves."

"Forget it," Burt replied. "That's the way it is."

A few hours later Dalton called Burt back. "Everything will remain exactly the way it is," he said. "Half the force has volunteered to work after hours without pay. The county and state cops have offered to help any way they can. The marshals want to pitch in. Everyone is up in arms about this. Would you believe that we just got a bulletproof vest for you from the Justice Department. The label on it says 'has not been fully qualified for ballistic penetration.' I suppose they give you your money back if it doesn't work."

"I appreciate the support," Burt said, "but I can't permit it. I'm not going to be treated as a charity case. There's a principle involved here. Just thank everyone for their kindness and make arrangements to withdraw the men."

Burt broke the news to Laurie that night. There was no rejoicing at the freedom she was about to get. "When the word gets out that we're alone," she said, "we could be in big trouble."

"Maybe," Burt told her, "but if anything happens to us, the world is going to know who's responsible. I'm going to hold a press conference tomorrow and announce what's happened. I'm going to ask whether under similar circumstances, they'd relocate Ted Kennedy to Ohio. I'm going to hold my press clippings in one hand and my bulletproof vest in the other. Let everyone know that this is the way the government encourages politicians to be honest."

Laurie shared Burt's anger, but she warned against going public. "If we don't make a big deal of this and don't go out a lot," she said, "maybe the word won't get out that we're alone. But if you have a press conference, you might as well send invitations to everyone who wants to hurt us."

Reluctantly, Burt accepted her advice. There was no press conference. The protection was withdrawn. Several cops continued to show up, as they put it, "just to say hello." Others insisted on giving Burt their home phone numbers in case anything came up. Carl Hirshman, the head of the Newark Marshals' Office, came to Fort Lee during his off hours to make sure the mayor was all right.

Less than twenty miles away, Jonathan Goldstein, Bruce Goldstein and Dick Shapiro had begun to shift their focus away from Burt Ross. For them, someone else had now taken over the limelight. He was their new star witness. His name was Arthur Sutton.

Sutton's claim that he had been the victim of extortion had lasted only until it became public that Burt's conversations with him had been taped. When transcripts of the tapes were given to the developer during pretrial disclosure, the extortion defense went out the window.

The previous August, on an afternoon when Burt and Laurie had been picking blueberries on Martha's Vineyard, Sutton and his attorney had arrived in Newark for an appointment with the U.S. Attorney. The developer told Jonathan Goldstein that he wanted to plead guilty, become a government witness and tell all. There was more to the case than the U.S. Attorney knew, he said. More than Burt Ross knew. A lot more.

And so there was. The story that Sutton laid out for Jonathan and his staff was just the break they had needed. In fact, Sutton's unexpected switch would make this the biggest case the U.S. Attorney had ever handled. It would shake an entire industry. And it would provide an intimate picture of how big business and a company linked with organized crime could work together when it served their mutual interest.

Throughout the late summer and fall, the U.S. Attorney sifted through thousands of documents he had subpoenaed from Investors Funding, pleaded with the Internal Revenue Service to provide accountants to help decipher the material and brought in real estate experts to familiarize him with a highly complex business. At first the enormity of what he was up

171

against seemed staggering. After months of round-the-clock research, the pieces started to come together.

To the general public, Arthur Sutton and the George Washington Shopping Plaza had been synonymous. The reality was something else. When Sutton had retired from Arlen Realty in 1970 with about a million dollars' worth of stock, he had begun looking for something else to do. He found it in Fort Lee.

Soon after he began acquiring land there in late 1971, word of his project spread and land prices soared. Within months, Sutton was in over his head. At Arlen he had been in charge of all construction. This was different. It was his money and he didn't have enough of it. It was a delicate, high-risk venture, and he didn't have the background to put it together. By the middle of 1972, he needed help fast.

The company Sutton turned to was perfectly suited for his needs. Investors Funding Corporation was listed on the American Stock Exchange, it claimed $379 million in assets and it was no stranger to Fort Lee. IFC owned both apartment buildings and land in town, and it understood the potential of the area. Yet there was nothing local about its holdings. The company's portfolio included shopping centers, industrial plants, apartment complexes and huge tracts of land from New England to Florida. It had acquired two banks in Ohio, and a life and two title insurance companies. A few years before it had owned the Boston Celtics basketball team. When it bought P. Ballantine & Sons, the brewing company, in 1969, IFC stock hit an all-time high of $47 a share.

Investors Funding had started off as a family business in the late 1940s. The three Dansker brothers, Norman, Jerome and Ralph, dealt originally in second mortgages. When they switched to first mortgages and construction financing, the business mushroomed and so did their status. They moved to plush headquarters on Fifth Avenue, their payroll swelled to a thousand and the Danskers became pillars of New York's Jewish society.

172

Some suggested that IFC's phenomenal growth during the 1960s was due more to inflation than brilliant business acumen. Throughout the decade the company bought everything on highly leveraged factors: It took on speculative properties for a minimum amount of cash, then turned them over for a quick profit. The philosophy worked fine in a bullish economy, but when the recession started in 1970, IFC found itself overextended. It was left with properties for which there were no buyers, properties with tremendous carrying costs. Overnight, IFC's holdings came into question. When it unloaded Ballantine in 1972, the company wrote off an estimated $60 million loss.

With all its complicated activities, IFC's major role continued to be as a mortgage broker. It operated as a conduit, or middleman, borrowing money from banks and then loaning it at higher interest rates to private developers who didn't have the credit lines to finance their own projects. There wasn't a real estate outfit in the country that wasn't familiar with IFC. There weren't too many developers who hadn't done business with them.

In June of 1972, Arthur Sutton became another client. He began meeting regularly with IFC officers, outlining his plans and financial needs. The IFC people liked what they heard. True, the property needed rezoning and the new mayor had just imposed a moratorium on high-rise construction. But they decided to go ahead anyway. They budgeted $11 million to buy the seventeen acres and began funding Sutton in August.

At first IFC charged Sutton thirteen percent interest and forced him to sign a personal guarantee to protect the loan. By November Investors Funding had taken an even greater interest in the project. It took it over, reducing Sutton to tenant status.

For Sutton, IFC meant essentially three men. They were Norman Dansker, the company's president and chairman of the board; Stephen Haymes, the executive vice president; and Donald Orenstein, a senior vice president. These were the men he worked with to put his project together.

At forty-eight, Norman Dansker was the youngest of the three brothers who started the business. By 1972, he was running the show. His public image was that of a likable gentleman. He had a dry sense of humor. He worked quietly in the background and was always in control of himself. What he lacked in brilliance, he made up for with hard work and meticulous attention to details.

Stephen Haymes had been brought over by Dansker from Ballantine, where Haymes had been president, and Dansker treated him like a son. Outwardly, the two were very different. Dansker had dropped out of St. John's; Haymes was a graduate of Wharton and Harvard Law School. Dansker had wavy gray hair, dressed conservatively and seemed unburdened by pretense; Haymes wore flashy clothes and was full of himself. He was curt. He pressed a buzzer to let people into his office.

Like Sutton and Serota, Donald Orenstein came from a poor background and had little formal education. He had worked for Haymes at Ballantine and come over to IFC with him. Some called him Haymes's right-hand man; others said he was his errand boy. Orenstein was the field man in the organization, a talented negotiator and the one with whom Sutton felt most comfortable. Yet Orenstein was never secure in his ability or power. When others complimented him, he often asked them to repeat it to Dansker and Haymes.

When it came to the good life, Sutton was in good company with his new friends at IFC. Sutton had his $750,000 house, helicopter and Rolls Royce. Dansker had recently moved his wife and two children into an Edward Durell Stone home on a 420-acre estate in Westchester County. The estate had a pool, a tennis court and barns. Dansker had even built a five-acre lake. Haymes and his wife were preparing for their second child by buying an expensive Fifth Avenue townhouse. The Orensteins and their three children lived elegantly on Long Island.

Less than six months after he began doing business with IFC,

Sutton learned that he wasn't the only one living over his head. Orenstein approached him for a favor. Steve Haymes had a slight cash shortage, he said. Could Sutton loan him $50,000? The money, he promised, would be repaid at the next closing, disguised as part of the funds IFC was giving Sutton to buy land for the Fort Lee project.

Sutton agreed and cashed a personal check. Over the next year, it became a regular habit. He put up another $75,000 in cash for Haymes and Orenstein. He paid $145,000 in bills for Dansker's lake, and another $45,000 to rennovate Dansker's barn. Whenever Sutton provided cash or paid a bill, he was reimbursed the next time IFC funded the project. Each time, the cost of the land acquisition rose by the amount that had been illegally channeled for Dansker's, Haymes's and Orenstein's personal use.

The system the three men worked out with Sutton benefited their company as well as themselves. On several occasions IFC sold Sutton property that was losing money and looked bad on its books. Each time Sutton was compensated for his losses at closings on the Fort Lee project. As long as the banks kept putting up money and the project was built, everyone would come out ahead.

The result of all this personal and corporate corruption was that a sum of nearly $5 million was listed under expenses for the George Washington Shopping Plaza that in fact had nothing to do with it. Property owners in the three-square-block area that the project was supposed to encompass added to the spiralling cost. As word spread that Sutton was buying, asking prices soared. The owner of a small dry-cleaning plant which was assessed at about $100,000 received $1.3 million to move his hangers somewhere else. The occupants of an old clapboard house worth $40,000 got a million to pull up stakes.

By the end of 1973, Sutton and his silent partners had acquired almost all the property, but the price tag, including the $5 million in kickbacks and other transactions, was now $32 million. Because of this, the smaller project Sutton had envisioned would no longer do. To maximize the inflated value of the land, IFC had to put up something bigger. Something much bigger.

In January of 1974, Arthur Sutton publicly announced the giant project IFC had put together. The public went wild. By the time the board of adjustment began hearings on the variance requests in March, the mayor had announced his opposition and Nathan Serota had organized hundreds of people to come out and protest.

Things went from bad to worse. A fourteen-bank consortium led by Chase Manhattan, which had given IFC a $71 million credit line, was refusing to advance any more and was pushing for prompt repayment of its loan. When the American Stock Exchange suspended trading on IFC stock in early April, shares were selling for about one dollar. And as Fort Lee's board of adjustment moved inexorably toward rejecting the project, rumors circulated that Investors Funding might fold.

Sutton and IFC were at the brink. Their personal fortunes and corporate existences now depended on getting the George Washington Shopping Plaza approved.

15

By the end of 1974, Investors Funding had filed for bankruptcy and Burt had turned his attention to the trial. With more than two months to go, the papers were already carrying stories. Because of all the publicity, the jury would be picked in another part of the state and sequestered in a Newark hotel. Judge Frederick Lacey, a former U.S. Attorney for New Jersey, was turning down requests that he disqualify himself from presiding because he had once called Valentine Electric a hoodlum-ridden company.

While Jonathan Goldstein and his staff were trying to figure out how to weave all the evidence they had into a story that a jury could understand, the defense attorneys were also busy. They barraged the court with motions for dismissal and severence. They combed through Burt's files at Borough Hall and L.F. Rothschild and traced his activities back to elementary school. Private detectives were snooping around Fort Lee, offering money to anyone who could provide them with damaging information on the mayor. One of the people they approached was a borough administrator whom Burt had just fired. They must have thought he would be a likely informer. His response was to report the incident to Burt and the U.S. Attorney.

As Burt heard more and more about the defense lawyers, he worried about how badly he would be attacked on cross-examination. He also developed a nervous cough.

In February, he shaved his beard, got a haircut and began going regularly to Newark to prepare for the witness stand. The final run-through came with just a few days to go. Jonathan Goldstein, pretending to be a defense attorney, threw questions at him. Burt fielded them so easily that he grew concerned.

"There's no way it's going to be as easy as this," he told Jonathan. "Why don't we switch roles. You be me and I'll be the defense attorney. Let me show you how it's done."

For twenty minutes Burt paced the floor, shaking his fist at the U.S. Attorney, his voice carrying into the corridor.

"Isn't it a fact that you and Arthur Sutton have known each other for years?" he shouted. "Do you really expect this jury to believe that two men who knew each other so well needed an intermediary to discuss a bribe? Isn't the real truth that you and Sutton conspired to shake down each and every defendant in this case?"

Jonathan laughed when Burt had finished his act. "I think you've been watching too much Perry Mason," he said. "And besides, what are you so nervous about? You haven't done anything wrong."

"I'll tell you what I'm so nervous about," Burt said, "I'm nervous about being crucified."

It has been suggested that the purpose of a trial is not to determine truth, but to establish which side has the better lawyers. If a defendant has enough money to spend on legal fees, the argument goes, he can gain acquittal regardless of the evidence.

The defendants in the Fort Lee bribery trial spared no expense. The attorneys they hired represented some of New York's best-known legal talent. One of the lawyers had won courtroom victories for Spiro Agnew and Jacqueline Kennedy Onassis. Another had successfully defended John Mitchell. Roy

178

Cohn's law firm was in on the act. There was a former federal judge; a former chief criminal prosecutor; and a former state prosecutor. Estimates of the combined legal fees started at $1 million.

Peter Fleming, Jr., who had defended John Mitchell and was now representing Warner Norton of Investors Funding, demonstrated his capability before the trial even started. Moments before jury selection began in Trenton on March 10, Jonathan Goldstein made a surprise announcement: In return for immunity from prosecution, Norton had switched sides and become a government witness.

It took a full day to screen three hundred potential jurors and settle on eight men and four women. Most of those chosen were middle-aged, blue-collar workers. They included a postal clerk, a tavern owner, a truck driver, a retired butcher, a product inspector, a transportation engineer, two housewives and an unemployed dental technician. Three of them were black. Some felt the defense team wanted to avoid a jury of their clients' real peers. It would be a difficult case, the reasoning went, and the less anyone understood the better. These sharp New York lawyers would try to run circles around the U.S. Attorney. They would talk the jury into helpless confusion.

After a day off for traveling and getting the jury set up in a guarded hotel, the trial began March 12 in a courthouse built during the Depression that was wedged between the Victorian Newark police headquarters and the modern Federal Building that housed the U.S. Attorney's Office.

U.S. District Court Judge Frederick Lacey, a tall, balding man with an imposingly somber presence and a reputation as one of the country's most brilliant jurists, ordinarily presided in a small, efficient courtroom. To accommodate the swarm of defendants, lawyers, spectators and press in this case, he moved to a large, wood-paneled courtroom with velvet drapes and an elaborate carved ceiling.

The six defendants and their thirteen attorneys sat behind

179

long tables to one side of the bench. There was so much confusion in identifying them that large placards had to be provided. The thirty-three-year-old U.S. Attorney sat closer to the jury box, straddled by his two younger assistants, the hulking Dick Shapiro and the diminutive Bruce Goldstein. Compared with the sheer numbers of their opposition, the prosecutors seemed like David up against Goliath.

From the beginning, Norman Dansker sat alone, impassive except for an involuntary facial twitch. Stephen Haymes and Donald Orenstein exchanged frequent whispers and shook their heads in apparent disbelief at the most damaging government testimony. Joe Diaco and Andy Valentine distinguished themselves from the others by wearing checkered jackets and colored shirts. Their lawyers referred to Diaco and Valentine as "the hard hats," and to the others as "the moneybags." Valentine ran one hand through his pompadour and scribbled furiously on a notepad. Diaco leaned back in his chair, his hands behind his head, and stared straight ahead. Nathan Serota, his toupee blending perfectly into gray muttonchop sideburns, sat to the rear, slumped in his chair, expressionless behind yellow-tinted metal-rimmed glasses.

The relatives sat in the front row of the spectator benches. Gloria Dansker, dressed in conservative elegance, glasses perched in her gray hair, sat quietly with her twenty-two-year-old daughter. Gail Haymes, black hair descending to her waist, wore striking pantsuits and sneered along with her husband. Elise Orenstein, whose modest appearance set her aside from the others, dispatched her daughter during recesses to give Daddy a kiss. Vivian Serota, dressed simply and stylishly in subdued wool suits, sat several rows away from the family's husky personal–chauffeur. Valentine's wife, a plain, heavyset woman, appeared only once. Diaco's son, who looked like he had been fashioned in his father's tough image, came from time to time.

Sprinkled elsewhere among the spectators were a number of

marshals who kept their eyes on several surly characters they referred to as "wise guys." Lawyers who had nothing to do with the case, students and courtroom personnel filed in and out. Several people from Fort Lee attended regularly. Roy Sampath shifted in his seat when his name came up in testimony. Dave Ross flew up from Florida and heatedly discussed defense strategies during lunch breaks.

The government's opening statement was concise. Speaking in a low monotone that was broken only by an occasional stutter, Jonathan Goldstein touched on the mass of evidence he said would prove that "this case is about men who believe that every difficulty can be solved by paying money. It is about men who act without regard to the legal consequences and without concern for the citizens of Fort Lee."

One by one the defense attorneys rose to remind the jury that the government would have to prove its case beyond a reasonable doubt. The most important fact to keep in mind, they told the jury, was that the key witness at this trial would be a man who had already confessed his guilt. Arthur Sutton, they contended, would be testifying for the sole purpose of staying out of jail.

Burt was the first government witness. He and Laurie had been placed in protective custody again for the trial. As marshals opened the courtroom doors, an expectant hush fell over the audience. Many were seeing the mayor for the first time, and strained forward to get a better look. Burt was wearing a gray suit and dark tie. He walked quickly to the front. As he passed the jury box, he seemed to be limping more than usual.

His voice was strong, his style relaxed. When Jonathan asked how many hours a week he worked for his $5,000-a-year mayor's salary, Burt smiled and said, "Much more than $5,000 worth." He answered questions by looking directly at the jury, as though he and they shared some special intimacy in this incredible story.

Burt was still on the stand when Jonathan passed out blue

headsets to the judge, jury, defendants, attorneys, court clerk and stenographer. Speakers were also provided for the spectators. For the next three hours, everyone sat transfixed, listening to the tapes of Burt cursing at Diaco after the blackmail threat, to Diaco telling the Mayor that "these deals don't come off so easy," to Sutton explaining the fine points of mixing concrete. Even Diaco seemed caught up in the show. When he heard himself offer Burt "a couple of blondes in East Orange that would make your hair stand," he broke out in a grin.

When the U.S. Attorney got to the $100,000 Burt had received, he turned to the rear of the courtroom and motioned. A marshal stood up, walked to the front and handed him the purple accordion folder. Opening it, Jonathan asked Burt what was inside. "A lot of cash," Burt said.

Jonathan then introduced the money as evidence and placed the folder on a table at such an angle that several wads of bills spilled out. For the rest of the afternoon, jurors kept looking over at what was more money than any of them had ever seen before.

Burt himself wasn't so sure how he had done as a direct witness. "I kept looking for a sign from the jurors," he said as he and Laurie ate sandwiches in the marshals' office, "but I couldn't get any reading. I have the feeling that this case may be too complicated for them to understand. God help me on cross-examination."

What helped was Burt's persuasive performance. Three of the defense attorneys didn't ask him a single question. A fourth merely wanted a clarification. Only Diaco and Valentine's lawyers made an attempt to discredit him.

"They really had the place covered, didn't they?" Diaco's attorney asked sarcastically about the FBI stakeout of the Forum Diner.

"I certainly hope they did," Burt said.

The attorney asked Burt if his singing "We're in the Money" after getting the $100,000 had been a signal to the FBI.

"As a matter of fact," Burt said, "it was a release of incredible nervous tension."

"Didn't you tell Diaco that when people wanted favors of you, you expected them to do business through your brokerage house?" the lawyer asked.

"Absolutely not," Burt said evenly. "That's a one-hundred-percent falsehood. It's a lie."

"In other words, you never told him that?" the attorney persisted.

"That's exactly what I mean," Burt replied. "I never said anything remotely similar thereto."

Valentine's lawyer asked a few questions which indicated how thoroughly the defense had investigated Burt's past. He wanted to know whether Burt hadn't been a resident of New York when he was elected. He inquired about Dave Ross's real estate holdings. He held up the campaign literature that had been distributed after the indictments and asked Burt if he hadn't used the case for "every personal, political advantage you can get."

Burt's answers were polite but firm. He made a conscious effort to control his temper. When the lawyer thanked him sarcastically for an answer, Burt offered a seemingly sincere "You're welcome." When he suggested that the mayor's memory seemed to have improved with time, Burt said, "My memory was fine then and my memory is fine now as to those events. I will never forget them as long as I live."

Throughout the questioning, Judge Lacey made it clear that he would not permit lawyers to intimidate a witness. His face reddened when Diaco's lawyer said, "Oh, come now, Mr. Ross," to one of Burt's answers. "I will not have any vituperation," Lacey snapped. "You will allow the witness to complete his answer, whether you like the answer or not."

Lacey was tough but even-handed. When Jonathan suggested once that the jury seemed tired and perhaps a recess was in order, Lacey appeared to count under his breath before barking that he alone would determine when the jury needed rest. "I'd give anything to see William Kunstler handle a case before this guy," a reporter whispered. "Only one of them would come out alive, and my money would be on Lacey."

Burt embraced Laurie in the hall after his hour and a half of cross-examination had ended. "I can't believe I got off that easy," he said. "Call your parents and tell them to start cooking. We're all going to celebrate."

For Burt, it was over. He would have liked to sit among the spectators for the rest of the drama, but witnesses were not permitted back in the courtroom. So each night he waited anxiously for his father to come home with a report.

Soon after Burt departed, Arthur Sutton entered. Some of the defendants' relatives hissed as he walked past them to the witness stand. A few of the defendants tried to catch his eye. Their attorneys seemed to be licking their chops. Sutton looked through them.

From the moment the developer was sworn in, Lacey had to keep instructing him to raise his voice. He answered most questions in the present tense. He asked frequently to see his date book. He drank a lot of water.

During the two days Jonathan had Sutton on direct examination, he led him meticulously through each detail of his past relationship with Investors Funding, leading up to the moment when both Sutton and IFC faced bankruptcy if Fort Lee's board of adjustment didn't change its mind and permit them to build their shopping center. It was at this point, Sutton testified, that he met a fellow named Andy Valentine, who was president of a company called Valentine Electric. Valentine said he could be of help with the problem in Fort Lee. On April 12, the two men met alone in Sutton's Englewood Cliffs office. Valentine did most of the talking. Sutton and IFC had a big problem getting the zoning passed, he said, adding that he had helped others get things from the mayor. And what did Valentine want? Nothing, he said. Just the chance to do all the electrical work for the Shopping Plaza when it was built. The contract, Sutton estimated, should be worth $10 million.

Nothing was decided at the meeting. Three days later, Sutton left for California. While in Palm Springs, he got a message from Valentine that $3.5 million would be needed to get the zoning passed. On his return to New Jersey, he got in touch with Donald Orenstein. By now, Sutton must have known enough about Investors Funding so that he didn't have to worry about offending anyone's morality. The question was how IFC would react to putting up so much money.

It was cheap, Orenstein said. Why, the interest on the loan for the land alone was more than that. But even more important, Orenstein said, was that unless the variances were granted, the project would go under and so would IFC. If that's what it took to keep the ship afloat, he told Sutton, "we'll get the money somewhere."

On April 24, Sutton met again with Valentine. This time the electrical contractor said they had two major problems. One was Nathan Serota's opposition to the project. The other was Burt Ross. The solution, he suggested, was to purchase Serota's apartment for $900,000, pay Ross $200,000 and spread around another $300,000. The total outlay, then, would be only $1.4 million, less than half Valentine's first estimate.

There was only one problem, Sutton told Valentine. He was still unsure how IFC would get that kind of money. "Don't worry," Valentine assured him, "Norman Dansker has all the money in the world."

That night Sutton met with Orenstein and Dansker, first at IFC's office and then for dinner at a nearby restaurant. Dansker was upset. The idea made sense, and they might be able to raise the $500,000 for the mayor and the others. But where would they get the $900,000 to pay Serota in one lump? Maybe Serota would agree to be paid in installments, Orenstein suggested.

Sutton called Valentine the following morning and asked

about spreading out the payments. Valentine said it wouldn't work. It had to all be up front. He would need a $900,000 certified check.

That same day, three candidates hand-picked by Serota filed to oppose the mayor's slate in the June 4 Democratic primary. Since the Republicans in Fort Lee were in disarray, the proposal on Serota and Ross, if accomplished, would cover both sides in the election.

On April 29, Sutton met Dansker and Haymes for dinner. First he pushed to regain his equity in the project. When Dansker agreed, the three men discussed the best way to handle the cash. Dansker wanted Sutton to funnel it. Sutton said Orenstein should do it. But as they debated the point and Sutton succumbed, it became clear that the real problem was how to raise the money in the first place.

For the next week, the phones were busy. Valentine kept asking when the cash would be ready. IFC and Sutton worried about how to generate funds through a closing. On May 6, Valentine came to Sutton's office and announced that the Serota deal was set. They would close on his apartment in four days. He would need the $900,000 certified check by then, and $300,000 in cash as well. The latter amount, he confided for the first time, was for Serota as well.

Sutton began scrambling. He cashed personal checks, took money from his company and borrowed from his sister and brother-in-law. Still he was unable to raise the $300,000 in cash for Serota, much less the $900,000 for the certified check. When he explained this during a surprise birthday party for Dansker at Club Cavallero on May 8, Haymes said there was only one solution: They would have to send Orenstein to the closing. Maybe he could reason Serota into accepting less up front. Orenstein was, after all, a shrewd negotiator. He had proved that by getting Fort Lee property owners to sell to Sutton after the developer himself had given up.

On May 10, the morning of the closing, Valentine called

Sutton and said he was sending over his chauffeur to pick up the cash. Sutton, who hoped that Orenstein would be able to work something out with Serota, didn't tell Valentine that he had only been able to raise $100,000. He just asked how he would be able to recognize the chauffeur. "He'll identify himself," Valentine said.

An hour later, a purple Lincoln pulled into the parking lot outside Sutton's office. A solidly built man with short black hair, a thick neck and a small scar over one eye entered the building.

"Andy sent me," he told Sutton.

"Are you his chauffeur?" Sutton asked.

"No," the man said. "I'm his partner. My name is Joey D."

Sutton handed him an envelope containing $100,000, and Diaco left without opening it. At the Manhattan office of Serota's attorney, Orenstein later told Sutton, Serota was furious because there was no certified check. The deal was off. The papers remained unsigned.

Sutton went to IFC's office that night to discuss picking up the pieces. Orenstein volunteered to go to Serota's apartment the next morning. Maybe Serota's temper would subside by then. And by the way, Orenstein asked, who was that guy at the closing who called himself Joey D.?

Sutton said Joey was on their side.

Well, whoever he was, Orenstein said with admiration, he sure was something. As Serota had ranted on at the meeting, Diaco had walked up to him, looked directly in his eyes and said "Shut up." And Serota had. It was the first time, Orenstein said, that he had seen anyone who was able to get the guy to calm down.

May 11 was a Saturday, but Sutton was in his office that morning when Valentine and Diaco walked in. Valentine was fuming. He had been made a fool of yesterday, he said. What kind of game was Sutton playing with him? Sutton told him not to worry, that he'd somehow raise the additional money. Valentine was not appeased. "I ought to wash my hands of this whole thing," he told Sutton as he stalked out with Diaco. "And remember one thing. I'm doing all this for nothing."

Sutton arrived at his home in nearby Alpine around noon and took his young son out on the front lawn to play ball. A few minutes later, a Rolls Royce pulled up his long driveway and parked next to the one he owned. Serota was behind the wheel. Orenstein was sitting next to him.

Sutton had never spoken with Serota before, but he had seen him voicing objections to the Shopping Plaza at the board of adjustment hearings. It was different now. Serota greeted Sutton warmly and invited him and his son into the car. Serota started to say something, but Sutton felt uncomfortable with his son sitting there holding his baseball bat. He asked the boy to leave.

Now they could talk man to man. Serota took them for a ride and did most of the talking. Orenstein had convinced him to take $200,000 in cash instead of $300,000, he said. And better yet, he would accept a certified check for $250,000 and a series of promissory notes at the closing instead of the $900,000 in one lump. "I really shouldn't do this," he told Sutton.

With the finances settled, Sutton and Serota began to talk about the board of adjustment hearings. "We can take care of the hearings," Serota said. "We'll cooperate with you." Their chat was interrupted when a cop pulled up next to them and waved Serota to the side. The cop asked Serota for his license. Serota said he had left it at home. When the cop recognized Sutton, he asked him to please do the driving until Serota left town.

Sutton called Orenstein that evening to congratulate him for bringing Serota around. "You did a great job," he told him. Orenstein thanked him for the praise. He had just one request to make. "Please call Dansker," he told Sutton. "Tell him what a good job I did."

On Monday, May 13, Sutton and his three IFC friends had breakfast together in Manhattan. Now that the glow had worn off Saturday's victory, they still had to figure out how to raise the money. Orenstein said they'd get it somehow. He called Sutton later in the day to report that the new closing on Serota's apartment had been set for Wednesday. Orenstein said he had only been able to come up with $150,000. Could Sutton somehow make up the difference? It was now or never for all of them. Sutton came through. He cashed company checks and borrowed some more from relatives. When he was still $60,000 short, he turned to a tenant in his building. The man's name was Anthony Carminati and he ran a company called 803 Maintenance Corporation. He told Sutton he could give him sixty, but it would cost the developer eighty to get it. Sutton agreed. A year later Carminati was arrested in a loan-sharking crackdown and described by police as a chief in the New York Mafia family of Carlo Gambino and the kingpin of New Jersey crime operations.

By Wednesday morning Sutton had put together his package and given it to Diaco. Orenstein had gotten his brother-in-law to take title to the apartment, since neither Investors Funding nor Plaza Associates wanted their names on the contract.

This time the closing went through without incident. Serota agreed in writing to halt his opposition to the project. He still had plenty of motivation. Payment on the promissory notes was contingent on approval of the Shopping Plaza.

The defense attorneys had Sutton on the stand for nearly a week. They challenged everything he said. They called him a liar. They demanded to know if he had made a deal with the government to stay out of jail. They suggested that he had concocted the whole story to protect friends and relatives. They referred to him sarcastically by his original name, Spinelo.

Under attack, the natural aggressiveness of a self-made man surfaced. Sutton's voice became stronger. His answers were more direct. He lashed out at allegations that he was a liar. Sure, he hoped for leniency from the court, he said, but every word of his testimony had been the truth.

At the beginning of the third week, the government made a crucial decision. It rested its case. It called neither Warner Norton, the IFC executive who had so recently switched sides, Councilman Mike Mosolino, the switchboard operator who had gotten Diaco's fingerprints, nor a single police officer or FBI agent.

"This is a very complicated case," one of Jonathan's assistants was overheard to say in the hall. "The way to lose it is by going into such detail that the jury gets confused."

"They've blown it," a defense attorney exclaimed jubilantly.

When the government rested, at least one element of the defense strategy had become clear. They were constantly assaulting Lacey with motions for a mistrial or for severence. In frequent conversations at the bench, they huddled before Lacey like a football team during a time out. Each time they rose to challenge him on the law, the jury was excused. With increasing urgency they argued that their clients couldn't possibly get a fair trial because it would be impossible for the jury to distinguish among them.

Lacey remained in his chambers each evening until well past midnight, searching for legal precedents and preparing opinions. He seemed resolute in his desire to shepherd the case through to a verdict.

A bomb dropped when Lacey asked the defense to present its case: It didn't call a single witness. Not one defendant took the stand. The government had failed to prove its case beyond a reasonable doubt, the lawyers asserted, and assumptions of guilt could not be applied to defendants who did not testify in their own behalf.

Some observers suggested another reason for the defense's decision: To put their clients on the stand would have exposed them to the possibility of being destroyed on cross-examination. And the government could have called Warner Norton as a rebuttal witness to knock down any concocted tales. In the intellectual move–countermove that was unfolding, the defense had decided not to take the gamble.

Shortly before summations, Lacey dismissed two of the three counts against Serota. There was no evidence, he concluded, that Serota was involved in the conspiracy to bribe Burt, or that he even knew about it in the first place. Serota and his wife were jubilant after the decision.

Defense summations took two days. Diaco's lawyer asked the jury to believe that his client had been a "poor fish" who had been lured into illegal acts by a mayor who had been the first to mention money. "Thank God," he concluded, "that in the United States a man such as Joseph Diaco can have his day in court, among his peers, where he is entitled to all of the protections that this fine country of ours can give him." The only reason Valentine had ever approached Sutton, his lawyer argued, was to apply for a mortgage. And as for Burt, "the evidence does not show that the mayor was any kind of hero. Reasonable doubt. That's what it's all about. Do justice. Tell them that Andy Valentine is not guilty."

Orenstein's attorney contended that his client was an innocent victim of Sutton's lies, that he had only been doing his job "while this undercurrent of criminal activity and attempted bribery was going on."

Haymes' and Dansker's lawyers emphasized that Burt had had no dealings at all with their clients. In fact, the government's entire case against them rested, as Dansker's lawyer put it, on "Mr. Sutton, a wily, corkscrew-minded fellow . . . shifty-eyed, beady-eyed. His first instinct is to sneak, and that is the kind of man on whom the government relies to convict the head of a major corporation."

Serota's lawyer was Martin London, a tall, handsome man with prematurely gray hair and a neatly clipped moustache. In his closing statement, he demonstrated why he had been retained by Spiro Agnew and Mrs. Onassis. Speaking flamboyantly, his arms gesticulating at the jury, London said his client

191

had sold his condominium only because he had grown weary of opposing Sutton's project and had decided to "get the devil out of town." There was no proof at all that Serota had gotten $200,000 in cash, he argued, and far from being a secret, illicit deal, the $900,000 apartment sale had been completed in "broad daylight," signed with contracts in a lawyer's office. Why, he himself had insisted on the contract's being introduced as evidence.

On top of that, London contended, Serota could be charged with bribery only because he was a public official. And he was a public official only because three years before, his former friend Burt Ross had insisted on appointing him to some insignificant body called the Fort Lee Parking Authority. When Serota had appeared before the board of adjustment to oppose the Sutton application, London stressed, it was as a private citizen, not as a government official. The Serota transaction may have raised some questions of morality, London concluded, but it was clearly not illegal, and "anybody who calls it a bribe is just trying to pin a label on it."

Jonathan took less than two hours to sum up. Speaking with little emotion, he went over each incriminating piece of evidence. What Serota's lawyer had neglected to mention, he emphasized, was that the contract on the sale of the apartment had a buy-back clause. Serota would have continued to live in it for a few years, paying only maintenance, and would then have repurchased it for only $300,000. The whole scheme was nothing more than a thinly-disguised plan to funnel money illegally.

"There's a common motive and a common theme to all these defendants," Jonathan concluded. "Make as much money as you can. Disregard the public concern."

"I'm worried about Goldstein's closing," one spectator whispered as Lacey charged the jury. "He touched all the bases, but his delivery was so matter-of-fact. I wonder how much of it got through to those twelve people sitting up there. Their faces seem so blank."

The jury retired to consider its verdict late on the afternoon of March 28. While it deliberated, four of the defendants dined nearby in an expensive restaurant. Dansker sat quietly at one table. Haymes and Orenstein talked loudly at another. When they got their check, they sent it over to Serota. "You got the $200,000 in cash," Orenstein laughed. "You pay for the dinner."

While the defendants dined, Burt and Laurie were also eating out. It was the eve of Burt's thirty-second birthday, but he was in no mood for festivities. He had heard that the jury was out, and he was nervous. "If they get off," he said, "it's all been for nothing. You can take everything I've done and throw it in the garbage. And my reputation along with it."

A few minutes before midnight, the jury sent word into the courtroom that it had reached a verdict. The trial had taken two and a half weeks. The jury was out for less than seven hours.

As the jurors filed into the box and took their seats, reporters raced in from the hall, the defendants leaned forward in their seats, their wives moved closer to each other. There was absolute silence. The curtain Burt Ross had lifted ten months before was about to drop.

Lacey asked the foreman to stand. "Referring to count one," he said, "how do you find as to the defendant Dansker?"

There was a slight pause, then it came. "Guilty."

"The defendant Haymes?"

"Guilty."

"The defendant Orenstein?"

"Guilty."

It sounded now like the steady drumbeat at a military funeral.

"The defendant Investors Funding?"

"Guilty."

"The defendant Valentine?"

"Guilty."

"The defendant Diaco?"

"Guilty."

"The defendant Valentine Electric?"

"Guilty."

Lacey turned to the second count. Each name was called. Each response was "Guilty." The prosecutors turned away as Mrs. Orenstein burst into tears and fled the courtroom.

"It can't be," Mrs. Haymes shouted.

"I'm ruined," Valentine sobbed.

Dave Ross knocked on his son's door at one-thirty. "I just got a call," he said. "The jury has reached a verdict."

One by one, his father named the defendants. One by one, he pronounced them guilty. After each name, Burt interrupted with "will you stop screwing around. What about Serota?"

Finally, Dave Ross came to the end of the list and looked down. "Nathan Serota," he said. "Guilty as charged."

Epilogue

On June 3, 1975, Judge Lacey sentenced all defendants in the Fort Lee bribery trial to five years in prison and fined them $10,000 on each count. For Nathan Serota, Lacey had special words.

"Your conduct was despicable," he said. "You not only showed an unconcealed contempt for the people of Fort Lee, you betrayed the government you are part of. You prostituted yourself and your cause. You were cunning. You were shrewd. You were greedy. And you were corrupt. You had no need for more money. You had all you could ever require. But your flabby morality would not allow you to pass up what must have seemed to you a heaven-sent opportunity to add to your immense wealth. You are the one defendant, had you been in the other counts, that I would have given serious consideration to imposing consecutive sentences on."

All the defendants appealed the verdict. On June 2, 1976, the U.S. Court of Appeals for the Third Circuit upheld the convictions on the bribe of Burt Ross and sent back for further consideration the convictions on the conspiracy count. It reversed Serota's only conviction so that he was acquitted and it reversed the convictions of the other defendants on the bribe of Serota. The Court stated that Serota did not have "any ability . . . to influence official decisions concerning the project in his official capacity, or that the alleged bribers believed he could do so by virtue of his public office." While the Court described Serota's motives in agreeing to sell his apartment as "hardly commendable," it held that Serota had not agreed to influence corruptly the Fort Lee board of adjustment and accordingly his conduct did not violate the New Jersey bribery statute.

Arthur Sutton was sentenced to six months in jail and fined $10,000. He entered federal prison on June 25, 1975, and was released just before Thanksgiving.

Investors Funding Corporation went bankrupt, leaving Chase Manhattan and the other banks to explain why they had sunk so many millions into a project that didn't even have the necessary variances.

The seventeen acres that Sutton and IFC had sought to build their fortunes on remained empty, a bulldozed eyesore with an uncertain future in the middle of a tired town.

In September of 1975, Burt Ross was appointed by the Governor of New Jersey to head the State Energy Office. He left his job at Rothschild, passed on the mayoralty to Councilman Dick Nest and bought an old Victorian house in a nearby town.

At his last meeting as mayor, a large crowd filed into Borough Hall to say good-bye. There was a standing ovation, gifts and embraces. When it came time to speak, Burt leaned toward the microphone and looked beyond the television cameras to these people he knew so well. "We have come a long way," he began, "from that day four years ago when we squeezed into an overcrowded headquarters on Main Street." Then his voice broke and he had to stop.